D1349329

Peter Gordon
EVERYDAY

Peter Gordon
EVERYDAY

PHOTOGRAPHY BY **MANJA WACHSMUTH**

jacqui
small

Everyday is dedicated to everyone who cooks at home using the best ingredients with an inquisitive mind. Manja brought the food to life with her gorgeous photography, Grant cooked half the book when I couldn't be there, and Lianne sourced many beautiful props. Ali and her team at HarperCollins asked me to write it in the first place and Sally at *House & Garden* continues to be a huge support. The teams in my restaurants in New Zealand and the UK have been incredibly accommodating as I tested the recipes, and Michael, as always, has been there 100 per cent. And Al, thanks for the chicken 'haere pie'!

First published in the UK in 2012 by
Jacqui Small LLP
An imprint of Aurum Press
7 Greenland Street
London NW1 0ND

First published by HarperCollins*Publishers (New Zealand) Limited* 2012

Text copyright © Peter Gordon 2012
Photography copyright © Manja Wachsmuth

Peter Gordon and Manja Wachsmuth, author and photographer, respectively, assert the moral right to be identified as the authors of this work.

Publisher: Jacqui Small
Project Editor: Abi Waters
Production: Peter Colley
Food styling by Grant Allen and Peter Gordon
Props courtesy of Melanie Roger Gallery (Martin Poppelwell platter on page 89), Masterworks Gallery (Katherine Smyth plates and bowls on pages 47, 101 [platter], 121, 167, 219 [black bowl] and 279, and Chris Weaver saucer on page 21 and plate on page 31), Lianne Whorwood of The Props Department, Grant Allen, and Manja Wachsmuth.
Cover and internals design by Kate Barraclough
Publisher: Alison Brook

ISBN: 978 1 906417 88 8

A catalogue record for this book is available from the British Library.

2014 2013 2012
10 9 8 7 6 5 4 3 2 1

Printed in China

TRANSLATION OF INTERNATIONAL COOKING TERMS

If you are unsure of an ingredient or cooking term used in any of the recipes, please refer to this general guide for international readers:

- If in any doubt of the type of cream to use, always use double.
- Unless otherwise specified, use plain flour.
- Unless otherwise specified, use caster sugar.

Other common terms and their translations:

- capsicums – peppers (red, green and yellow)
- eggplant – aubergine
- cinnamon quill – cinnamon stick
- baking soda – bicarbonate of soda
- vanilla bean – vanilla pod
- tomato paste – tomato purée
- skillet – frying pan or griddle
- pot – saucepan
- stick blender – hand-held blender
- plastic wrap – cling film

| CHAPTER ONE |

BREAKFAST AND BRUNCH

Apologies for this long recipe – but I thought you should learn to make hollandaise sauce, which is easier than you think!

POTATO RÖSTI WITH POACHED EGGS, BACON AND HOLLANDAISE FOR 4

150 g butter, melted and kept warm in a
    small jug at the back of the stove
3 tbsp lemon juice
10 eggs
1 tbsp hot water
2 litres water
100 ml white wine vinegar or cider
    vinegar, for poaching
3–4 large potatoes (about 900 g)
1 handful picked flat parsley
3 tbsp snipped chives
salt and freshly ground black pepper
butter or oil, to fry
8 rashers bacon

1. Preheat oven to 100°C.

2. First make the hollandaise. Make sure the butter is warm. Choose a metal bowl that will fit inside a slightly smaller diameter saucepan and bring 3 cm of water to a rapid simmer – it's important that the bottom of the bowl doesn't touch the water as it could curdle the sauce.

3. Place the lemon juice, 1 whole egg and 1 egg yolk in the bowl.

4. Whisk the egg mixture in the bowl over the simmering water – you can set it at a gentle boil so long as you whisk it continuously.

5. Once the egg begins to thicken, resembling lightly whipped cream, take the saucepan off the heat and then very slowly drizzle in the warm butter, whisking continuously until it has all been emulsified. Lastly, whisk in 1 tbsp very hot water, which will help stabilize it.

6. Keep covered in a warm place while you finish the dish.

7. Fill a deep pot with at least 2 litres of water and bring to the boil. Add 100 ml white vinegar or cider vinegar per 2 litres water, put the lid on and keep at a simmer. (Note: never add salt when poaching eggs.)

8. Peel the potatoes and grate on a coarse grater, squeezing out as much liquid as you can and mix potato with the parsley and half the chives. Season with salt and pepper. Divide the mixture into four.

9. Heat a pan with a little butter or oil over moderate heat. Press each mound of potato, which should be smaller than a saucer, firmly into the pan to keep the rösti tight. Cook until golden, then carefully flip over and cook on the other side. If not cooked through when golden they can be finished in the oven.

10. Grill or fry the bacon and keep warm in the oven.

11. To poach the eggs, bring the pot of water back to a gentle boil and move the pot just off centre on the element. Give the water a stir to create a gentle whirlpool, then crack an egg into a cup and gently drop it into the water. Cook the remaining eggs the same way, working quite quickly so all the eggs are cooked to the same degree – they take around 4 minutes. Use a slotted spoon to remove the eggs to a warm shallow dish.

12. To serve, sit a rösti on a warmed plate, lay the bacon across and sit two eggs on top. Give the hollandaise a gentle whisk then spoon it over and sprinkle with the reserved chives.

More often than not this classic North African dish (which is now also a classic of modern Israel thanks to the Tunisian Jews who settled there) is vegetarian and, much as I am happy to eat it that way, I prefer this spiced-up version containing lamb – although simply omit it if you prefer.

LAMB SHAKSHOUKA FOR 4

3 tbsp olive oil

¼ tsp cumin seeds

½ tsp sesame seeds

2 onions, peeled and thinly sliced

2 red capsicums, deseeded and sliced

2 cloves garlic, peeled and chopped

¼ tsp paprika or cayenne pepper

150 g minced lean lamb (optional)

salt

6 ripe tomatoes, diced (or 1 x 400 g tin chopped tomatoes and a little tomato paste)

4 eggs

50 ml plain yoghurt

1 small handful picked parsley, mint and coriander

1. Ideally you want to serve this in the dish you cook it in, so a large frying pan with a lid is good. Heat up the pan and add the olive oil, cumin and sesame seeds.

2. Once they begin to sizzle, add the onions, capsicums, garlic and paprika or cayenne pepper. Sauté until the vegetables collapse, stirring frequently.

3. Add the mince (if using) and a little salt. Cook until the lamb crumbles, stirring all the time.

4. Add the tomatoes and bring to a boil, then cook over moderate heat for 6–8 minutes, at which point much of the juice will have evaporated.

5. Make four impressions in the mixture and break an egg into each 'hole'.

6. Spoon the yoghurt on, put a lid on the pan and cook until the eggs have begun to set, but still have runny yolks.

7. Scatter with the shredded herbs and serve immediately straight from the pan.

This simple breakfast dish is based on the tasty Spanish Pan con Tomate *(also known as* Pan a la Catalana)*, which is much like Italian bruschetta but with tomato rubbed on as well. Often eaten as a snack, it makes a great base for a breakfast 'fry-up' with a Spanish theme – just make sure the tomatoes are really ripe so they collapse on the toast.*

CHORIZO AND EGG ON TOMATO-RUBBED TOAST FOR 4

4 eggs
500 g cooking chorizo, peeled and
    sliced 1 cm thick
extra virgin olive oil
4 slices good, firm bread (like
    sourdough)
1–2 cloves garlic, peeled
2 very ripe tomatoes, cut in half
2 handfuls salad leaves

1. Soft-boil the eggs – cook in a pot of boiling water for 4 minutes, then place in iced water (or under cold running water) for a few minutes and peel them.

2. Sauté the sliced chorizo in a little olive oil until golden and sizzling, then keep warm.

3. Toast the bread and rub one side with the garlic. Drizzle each slice with 1 tsp olive oil and rub the tomato into it, crushing it as you go (hence the need for firm bread – white fluff will break up). The end result is mashed tomato on bread.

4. To serve, pile on the salad leaves, eggs cut in half, chorizo and cooking fats – delicious!

This makes a lovely weekend brunch dish, but for a simpler breakfast dish serve the fritters with grilled, thickly cut bacon or sausage. If you can't find fresh cherries, canned or frozen ones also work really well.

CHERRY FRITTERS WITH SMOKED CHICKEN AND TOMATOES **FOR 6**

120 g flour
30 g polenta
¾ tsp baking powder
¼ tsp baking soda
¼ tsp smoked paprika
1 tsp sugar
¼ tsp salt
2 eggs
150 ml buttermilk or plain yoghurt
extra virgin olive oil
1 spring onion, thinly sliced
200 g cherries, pitted and halved
butter or vegetable oil, for frying
300 g smoked chicken, thinly sliced (or any other smoked meat or fish)
2 generous handfuls salad leaves
200 g cherry tomatoes, halved
1 tbsp lemon juice
salt and pepper

1. Preheat oven to 100°C.

2. Sift the first 7 dry ingredients and place in a bowl, making a well in the centre.

3. Beat the eggs and buttermilk or yoghurt with 1 tbsp extra virgin olive oil and pour into the well. Gently whisk the mixture together, then stir in the spring onion and cherries. Leave to rest for 15 minutes.

4. Place a heavy-based pan over moderate heat and add a generous knob of butter or oil until it sizzles.

5. Give the batter a stir, then drop large soup-spoonfuls of it into the pan and cook over moderate heat until they turn golden on the bottom and begin to firm up. Carefully flip over and cook the other side until cooked through. Cover with foil and keep warm in a low oven while you cook the rest.

6. To serve, divide the fritters between six plates and lay the sliced chicken over them. Toss the salad leaves and cherry tomatoes with the lemon juice, a few tablespoons of olive oil and a little salt and pepper. Pile on top of the fritters.

*Nothing beats a good scone – and these are all the better as they're full of flavour from
the cheese and bacon. They keep for a few days in an airtight container; reheat wrapped
in baking paper in the oven for 4 minutes to re-energize them.*

BACON AND CHEESE SCONES

MAKES 8 SCONES

100 g smoked streaky bacon lardons or thickly sliced bacon, diced

60 g butter, chilled, cut into small dice (plus an extra 25 g, melted, for finishing)

360 g flour

1½ tbsp baking powder

½ tsp cayenne pepper

2 spring onions, thinly sliced

80 g Cheddar cheese, coarsely grated (also try chunks of feta or Brie)

280 g buttermilk or plain yoghurt

1. Preheat oven to 200°C. Line a baking tray with baking paper.

2. Sauté the bacon in a knob of the butter until caramelized and slightly crisp – leave to cool but drain the fat from it and keep that, too.

3. The quickest way to make these scones is using a food processor, although you can make it easily enough by rubbing the fats in with your fingers. Place the flour, baking powder and cayenne pepper in the processor and blitz for 2 seconds.

4. Add the butter and reserved bacon fat, and pulse until it resembles crumbs. Tip into a large bowl and mix in the bacon, spring onions and cheese.

5. Make a well in the centre and gently mix in the buttermilk or yoghurt until a soft dough is formed – don't overwork it.

6. Dust your bench heavily with flour. Place the mixture on the bench and dust with more flour. Using a rolling pin, form a rectangle approximately 20 cm x 25 cm – it doesn't have to be exact. Cut in half lengthways and then each half into four to give you eight scones.

7. Place on the baking tray, quite close together, and brush with the melted butter.

8. Bake in the centre of the oven for 13–16 minutes until risen and golden.

9. Take from the oven, cool for a few minutes then transfer to a cake rack, although they're great eaten straight from the oven split in half and generously buttered.

These apples make a really good start to the day as they're slightly tart yet rich as well. I like to use a firm, slightly sour apple like a Granny Smith. Running your knife around the apple helps stop it splitting while it cooks.

APPLES STUFFED WITH TOASTED OATS AND HONEY FOR 4

60 g unsalted butter (plus extra for finishing)
80 g rolled oats
1 tsp ground cinnamon
2 tsp lemon juice
2 tbsp honey
4 firm apples
yoghurt and fresh berries, to serve

1. Preheat oven to 170°C.

2. Heat the butter in a frying pan until it goes foamy. Add the oats and cook them until golden, stirring constantly to prevent burning. Add the cinnamon, lemon juice and honey, cook for 20 seconds then take off the heat.

3. Remove the stem from the apples and sit them with their fattest end facing down on a board. Using a melon baller or small teaspoon, scoop out the seeds and core but don't go all the way through or the stuffing will fall out.

4. Run a small sharp knife around the apple's circumference, just cutting through the skin.

5. Stuff the apples with the oats and sit them on a baking tray lined with baking paper. Put a knob of butter on top of each one and bake until you can insert a thin skewer through the apple towards the centre with little resistance.

6. Serve warm with yoghurt and berries.

A great start to the day, this will give you some bounce in your step.

RASPBERRY, BANANA AND AVOCADO SMOOTHIE FOR 2

1 punnet (2 handfuls) raspberries
1 banana, peeled and broken into pieces
1 avocado, flesh only
300 ml buttermilk or plain yoghurt
   (cold from the fridge)
2 tbsp active manuka honey (or any
   other runny honey)
1 tbsp toasted muesli or bran flakes
   (optional but it gives it great body)
1 glass ice cubes

Place everything in a blender and blitz for 20 seconds. Taste and add extra honey or ice as needed.

I think of this as an autumn drink because of the cooked pears, although it's delicious all year round. You can cook the pears up to three days in advance and keep them in the fridge. Try replacing the kiwifruit with a peeled banana or mango, or figs if they're in season.

PEAR AND KIWIFRUIT LASSI FOR 4

2 pears, peeled, cored and cut into chunks
4 tbsp maple syrup or honey
zest and juice of 1 lemon
200 ml water
3 kiwifruit, peeled and cut into chunks
600 ml thin plain yoghurt
2 handfuls ice cubes

1. Place the pears, maple syrup or honey, lemon zest and juice and the water in a pan and bring to a boil. Put a lid on and simmer until the pears are cooked through – about 15 minutes. Leave to cool in the pan until needed.

2. Place the pears and cooking liquid along with everything else into a blender and blitz until smooth.

You can use either hot-smoked or cold-smoked salmon, and the goat's cheese can be replaced with most other cheeses.

SMOKED SALMON AND GOAT'S CHEESE OMELETTE FOR 2

5 eggs
1 handful flat parsley, coarsely
    shredded
4 tbsp cold water
salt and pepper
2 knobs butter (or 1 tbsp olive oil)
100 g smoked salmon, sliced or flaked
80 g goat's cheese, crumbled (or your
    favourite cheese)
hot buttered toast, to serve

1. Crack the eggs into a bowl. Add the parsley and the cold water. Season with salt and pepper and use a fork to beat the eggs for barely 4 seconds to break the yolks.

2. Place a 15–24 cm frying pan (ideally non-stick) over medium-high heat.

3. Add half the butter (or oil) and when it begins to sizzle pour in half the eggs. Swirl it around a bit and use a spoon or spatula to bring the set outer egg into the centre until it all begins to set.

4. Lay half the salmon and half the cheese across the centre and leave for another 5 seconds. Carefully fold one edge over the filling, then gently flip the omelette over. Give it a few more seconds, then slide onto a hot plate while you cook the other one.

5. Serve immediately with hot buttered toast.

I loved eating these as a child in my hometown of Whanganui – and although we never had them for breakfast or brunch (I didn't even know what brunch was until my late teens), I have served them as such in latter years. They're also a great supper dish served with salad, and are perfect for kids' parties.

SPAGHETTI AND CHEESE BREAD TARTLETS **MAKES 8 TARTLETS**

60 g melted butter (you may need more)
8 thin or medium slices white sandwich
   bread, crusts removed
1 x 400 g tin spaghetti in tomato sauce
50 g Cheddar-style cheese, grated

1. Preheat oven to 180°C.

2. Butter an 8-hole patty pan tin (or use muffin tins) and place in the freezer for 1 minute to set the butter. Press the bread firmly into each cavity and brush with the remaining butter, making sure you use it all up.

3. Spoon the spaghetti in and top with the cheese.

4. Bake until the bread is crisp and golden; around 20 minutes. Leave in the tin for a few minutes before removing. They're lovely eaten hot or cold.

My step-mum Rose's bacon and egg pie is legendary. I began making it in smaller tart sizes years ago to enable people to have an individual one so they didn't need to share. It's also great made with smoked chicken instead of bacon, and a thick slice of tomato on the top, before it's cooked, is terrific too.

ROSE GORDON'S BACON AND EGG TARTS

MAKES 6 x 10 cm TARTS OR 1 x 24 cm TART

50 g butter (plus extra for buttering)
500 g puff pastry
1 large white onion, peeled and sliced
300 g smoked bacon lardons or thick
   streaky bacon rashers, cut into batons
1–2 cloves garlic, crushed
120 g peas (frozen or fresh)
9 eggs
200 ml cream
salt and freshly ground black pepper
60 g grated Parmesan, Gruyère or
   Cheddar-style cheese

1. Preheat oven to 180°C. Butter six 10 cm diameter loose-bottomed tart tins (or one 24 cm tart tin) and chill in the fridge for 5 minutes. Roll out the pastry to 4 mm thick then press it firmly into the tins, trim and rest in the fridge for 20 minutes. Prick the bases of the tarts with a fork, line with baking paper and fill with baking beans. Place on a baking tray and blind bake for 15–20 minutes until golden. Leave for 5 minutes then remove the paper and beans.

2. Heat up a frying pan and cook the butter to a nut-brown colour. Add the onion and cook until caramelized. Add the bacon and garlic and cook until the bacon has softened. Mix in the peas, then take off the heat and divide half the mixture among the cooked tart shells.

3. Crack 3 eggs into a bowl, add the cream, season well with salt and pepper, then beat with a fork for 10 seconds. Stir in the remaining bacon mixture and divide this among the tart shells.

4. Crack an egg into the centre of each tart, sprinkle with the cheese and bake until the egg mixture is set; about 20–25 minutes. Leave to rest in the tins for 15 minutes before unmoulding. Can be eaten hot or at room temperature.

If you like, you can omit the bacon and use hot-smoked salmon or other fish instead, or use smoked paprika and increase the onions to two.

BAKED TOMATOES STUFFED WITH BACON, EGG AND SPINACH **FOR 4**

4 beefsteak tomatoes, or similar large tomatoes

1 onion, peeled and thinly sliced

2 tbsp extra virgin olive oil or butter

200 g smoked bacon lardons or thick streaky bacon rashers, cut into batons

80 ml cream

100 g spinach, washed and patted dry (if the leaves are large shred them, if using baby spinach leave whole)

4 eggs

2 tbsp snipped chives

salt and freshly ground black pepper

buttered toast, to serve

1. Preheat oven to 180°C. Line a baking tray with baking paper.

2. Cut the tomatoes in half horizontally, then using either a melon baller or a teaspoon with a good edge on it, scoop out all of the seeds and any fleshy membranes, leaving a lovely hollowed-out shell. Place the tomato halves on the baking tray, discarding the seeds and membranes.

3. Caramelize the onion in the oil or butter, stirring frequently, then add the bacon and cook until coloured.

4. Add the cream and bring to a simmer, then add the spinach.

5. Beat the eggs and chives with salt and pepper, then tip the bacon mixture on top and mix it in. Ladle the eggy mixture into the tomato halves and bake for about 10–12 minutes, at which point the egg will be setting.

6. Take from the oven and leave to rest for a few minutes. Carefully lift off the tray with a fish slice and serve immediately with lots of buttered toast.

The pikelet mixture works best if left to rest overnight, as a sort of sourness develops in it. If you don't have the time, just add 1 tsp baking powder to the flour. You can serve this topped with fresh sliced figs or Fig and Blueberry Compote (see page 32).

BLUEBERRY PIKELETS WITH FIGS AND VANILLA CRÈME FRAÎCHE FOR 6

3 eggs, beaten
320 ml milk
200 g plain flour
90 g butter, melted (plus extra for cooking)
salt
150 ml crème fraîche
¼ tsp vanilla extract
1 punnet blueberries, gently rinsed and patted dry
Fig and Blueberry Compote (see page 32), to serve
6 sweet ripe figs (optional)

1. Whisk the eggs with the milk.

2. Sift the flour into a bowl and make a well in the centre. Whisk in the eggs and milk, gradually at first, so as to make a lump-free batter. Cover with plastic wrap, poke a few holes in it with a toothpick and place in a cool, dark place for at least 3 hours or ideally overnight.

3. When you're ready to cook the pikelets, whisk in the melted butter and a pinch of salt.

4. Preheat oven to 100°C.

5. Mix the crème fraîche and vanilla together.

6. Heat a frying pan (ideally non-stick) to moderate heat, add a knob of butter and leave it to sizzle. Pour in spoonfuls of the batter and scatter blueberries on top. Make the pikelets whatever size you like.

7. Cook until the batter begins setting in the centre, then carefully flip them over and cook on the other side until just set. Remove from the pan and place on a tray in the oven while you cook the rest.

8. To serve, drizzle with Fig and Blueberry Compote (See page 32) and serve the crème fraîche on the side. Alternatively, slice the figs and scatter over the pikelets, then dollop on the crème fraîche.

FIG AND BLUEBERRY COMPOTE FOR 6

This is also lovely drizzled on French toast or ice cream.

4 dried or fresh figs, stalks removed, thinly sliced
100 g blueberries
50 ml maple syrup
2 tbsp lemon juice and 1 strip lemon peel

Place everything in a small saucepan and slowly bring to a simmer. Cook for 5 minutes to thicken.

These tropical fritters, much like pikelets, make for a lovely sweet brunch dish. You can also scatter diced melon over them, or chunks of mango.

BANANA AND COCONUT FRITTERS WITH PASSION FRUIT SAUCE **FOR 4-6**

130 g self-raising flour

1 tsp caster sugar

30 g desiccated coconut, lightly toasted

2 eggs

80 ml plain yoghurt

500 ml unsweetened coconut milk

3 tbsp grated dark palm sugar, brown
sugar or maple syrup

2 passion fruit, pulped

oil or butter, for cooking

2 bananas, peeled and sliced

1. Sift the flour and sugar into a bowl, mix in half the desiccated coconut and make a well in the centre. Whisk together the eggs, yoghurt and 250 ml coconut milk, then beat this into the flour to make a batter. Leave to rest for 15 minutes.

2. Preheat oven to 100°C.

3. Put the sugar or syrup and passion fruit pulp in a small pan and bring to a simmer. Add the remaining desiccated coconut and coconut milk and bring to a boil, then rapidly simmer for about 8 minutes until thickened. Keep warm.

4. Heat up a non-stick pan and brush with a little oil or butter.

5. You can make the fritters as large or as small as you like. Drop spoonfuls of the batter into the pan, laying some sliced banana on top. Cook for about 1½ minutes before carefully flipping over and cooking for another minute or so.

6. Remove from the pan, place in the oven on a baking tray lined with baking paper and finish cooking the remaining batter.

7. To serve, stack a few fritters on each plate and pour over the warm sauce.

A great brunch meal served with grilled bacon or black pudding. The pies are also really good served as a supper snack with a green salad.

SWEET POTATO, SPINACH AND CHEESE PIES **MAKES 4 x 10 cm PIES OR 1 x 24 cm PIE**

1 tbsp soft butter
300 g short crust pastry (see page 176),
    4 mm thick
1 large sweet potato (about 300 g),
    peeled and cut into 1 cm dice
300 g spinach, shredded, or whole baby
    spinach leaves
2 eggs
80 g grated cheese (Cheddar, feta or
    Parmesan)
2 spring onions, thinly sliced
salt and freshly ground black pepper
4 tbsp crème fraîche

1. Preheat oven to 180°C. Butter four 10 cm diameter loose-bottomed tart tins (or one 24 cm tart tin) and chill in the fridge for 5 minutes. Cut the pastry to fit the tins, press it in firmly, then rest in the fridge for 20 minutes. Prick the bases of the tarts with a fork, line with baking paper and fill with baking beans. Place on a baking tray and blind bake for 15–20 minutes until golden. Leave for 5 minutes then remove the paper and beans.

2. Meanwhile, steam or boil the sweet potato in salted water until almost cooked. Add the shredded spinach and cook for 30 seconds to wilt, then drain in a colander.

3. Beat the eggs with the cheese and spring onions and season with salt and pepper.

4. Mix in the sweet potato mixture, then spoon into the tart shells and drizzle the crème fraîche over each one.

5. Bake in the centre of the oven for 20–30 minutes until the filling is set.

6. Eat either straight from the oven or leave to cool a little before taking from the tart tins.

These scones make a perfect brunch dish – although they're equally good for a picnic bite. Balsamic butter goes really well with ham carved off the bone, and it's also lovely dolloped onto boiled new potatoes and sweet corn.

PARMESAN PINE NUT SCONES WITH BALSAMIC BUTTER, PROSCIUTTO AND TOMATO **MAKES 6 SCONES**

180 g butter (100 g straight from the fridge, diced, and 80 g at room temperature)

240 g flour, sifted

50 g Parmesan, grated

1 tbsp baking powder

1 good pinch fine salt

1 tsp sugar

50 g pine nuts

180 ml buttermilk (plus extra for brushing)

1 tbsp aged balsamic vinegar or balsamic glaze

¼ tsp flaky sea salt

8–12 slices prosciutto

2–3 tomatoes, sliced

1. Preheat oven to 200°C. Line a baking tray with baking paper.

2. Place the 100 g cold butter in a food processor. Add the flour and Parmesan and pulse until it resembles breadcrumbs.

3. Add the baking powder, salt and sugar and pulse for 2 seconds.

4. Tip onto your bench, make a well in the centre and add the pine nuts and buttermilk. Gently mix until it just comes together – overworking the dough makes the scones tough.

5. Dust the dough lightly with a little extra flour and roll out to give you a slab 2½ cm thick. Using a cookie-cutter or a knife, cut out 6 even-sized scones (any shape you like) and place on the baking tray.

6. Brush with the extra buttermilk and bake for 13–15 minutes until risen and coloured on top.

7. While they're cooking, beat the balsamic vinegar or glaze into the 80 g softened butter until emulsified, then mix in the flaky sea salt.

8. Once cooked, leave the scones on the baking tray for a few minutes before moving to a cake rack to cool.

9. To serve, split the cooled scones in half and spread both halves with the balsamic butter. Tuck in the prosciutto and sliced tomato.

This dish is based on the now-famous Changa restaurant's Turkish Eggs that are on the breakfast menus of my London restaurants and are a great way to start the weekend. Haloumi cheese is a firm salty cheese, originating from Cyprus, but it can be replaced with feta.

FRIED HALOUMI AND SPINACH WITH GARLIC YOGHURT, CHILLI BUTTER AND POACHED EGGS **FOR 4**

200 g haloumi, cut into 4 or 8 slices, depending how thick each piece is

1 clove garlic, finely grated

150 g thick Greek-style yoghurt

4 tbsp extra virgin olive oil

50 g unsalted butter

¼ tsp dried chilli flakes (more or less, to taste)

1 heaped tbsp snipped dill

200 g spinach, washed to remove grit and kept moist

salt and freshly ground black pepper

8 eggs

1. If the haloumi is very firm and salty, you can improve it by placing the slices in a bowl and covering with very hot water for 1 hour. Remove from the water and pat dry.

2. Whisk the garlic and yoghurt with half the olive oil and put to one side.

3. In a small pan over moderate heat, cook 30 g butter until it turns a pale nut-brown, take off the heat, add the chilli and swirl it around so it sizzles. Stir in the remaining olive oil and the dill and put to one side. Keep warm.

4. Heat up a wide frying pan and add the remaining butter. When it's sizzling add the spinach, toss it around until it wilts, and season with plenty of freshly ground black pepper and a little salt. Tip into a colander over a bowl and keep warm. Wipe the pan out and put back on the heat.

5. Drizzle 2 tsp oil into the pan. Lay in the sliced haloumi, keeping slightly separate, and cook until golden brown. Gently flip over and cook until golden on the other side, then turn the heat off and return the drained spinach to the pan.

6. Poach the eggs as described on page 10.

7. To serve, place the haloumi and spinach on four warmed plates. Sit two poached eggs on top, dollop with the garlic yoghurt and then drizzle with the still-warm chilli butter.

Absolutely delicious. Use any cheese you have: a soft goat's cheese, firm Cheddar or Gruyère, or even a blue.

PORTOBELLO MUSHROOMS STUFFED WITH CHEESE AND CHORIZO **FOR 4**

8 portobello mushrooms
100 g cheese, crumbled or grated
150 g cooking chorizo, skin removed, diced
2 cloves garlic, peeled and sliced
1 tsp fresh thyme leaves (or any herb of your choice)
80 g coarse fresh breadcrumbs or Japanese panko crumbs
2 tbsp olive oil, plus a little extra
salt and freshly ground black pepper
2 handfuls salad leaves
a little lemon juice or balsamic vinegar

1. Preheat oven to 180°C. Line a baking dish or roasting dish with baking paper.

2. Remove stalks from the mushrooms and sit the caps, gills facing up, on the tray.

3. Thinly slice the stalks and place in a bowl with the cheese, chorizo, garlic, thyme, breadcrumbs, 1 tbsp olive oil and some salt and pepper. Mix together to give a crumble-like consistency.

4. Divide the filling among the caps, piling it up, and drizzle with the remaining oil.

5. Bake in the centre of the oven for 15–20 minutes, at which point the caps will have collapsed a little and the stuffing will be sizzling away.

6. To serve, place two mushrooms per portion on warmed plates, drizzle on the cooking juices and pile salad leaves to the side. Drizzle the leaves with a little extra olive oil and lemon juice or balsamic vinegar as you prefer.

| CHAPTER TWO |

SOUPS

This chunky soup is very light and flavoursome, but does rely on all the vegetables being very thinly sliced. The salmon adds a wonderful elegance to the dish.

FENNEL, COURGETTE, PEA AND LETTUCE SOUP WITH SMOKED SALMON FOR 4

2 heads fennel, thinly sliced

2 x 15 cm stalks celery, thinly sliced

30 g butter

2 courgettes, cut into quarters
   lengthways then thinly sliced

3 spring onions, thinly sliced

2 baby gem lettuces or baby cos, leaves
   separated, washed and shredded

100 g peas (fresh or frozen), blanched
   and refreshed

200 ml single cream

600 ml chicken or vegetable stock

salt and pepper

100 g sliced smoked salmon, cut into
   5 mm strips

1 tbsp fresh dill sprigs

1. Sauté the fennel and celery over moderate heat in the butter without colouring. Once they begin to wilt, put a lid on and cook for 10 minutes, stirring occasionally.

2. Add the courgette, spring onion, lettuce, peas, cream and stock and bring to the boil. Cook over a gentle heat until the peas are cooked, about 5 minutes, stirring occasionally.

3. Season with salt and pepper, then ladle into four hot bowls. Place the salmon on top and sprinkle with the dill.

This easy-to-make soup is a great winter warmer. If you're not keen on dicing the carrot and potato, you can grate them or blitz in a food processor for a rustic look.

CREAMY LEEK, RED LENTIL AND POTATO SOUP **FOR 6**

50 g butter
1 leek, rinsed and sliced
1 carrot, peeled and diced
1 large potato, peeled and diced
2 bay leaves
1 litre vegetable or chicken stock
80 g red lentils, briefly rinsed under cold water
2 tbsp fresh oregano leaves (or 1 large tsp dried oregano)
100 ml plain yoghurt or cream
salt and freshly ground black pepper
1 handful picked flat parsley leaves

1. Cook the butter in a pot until it turns nut-brown.

2. Add the leek, carrot, potato and bay leaves and sauté for 5 minutes, stirring occasionally.

3. Add the stock, lentils and oregano and bring to the boil. Maintain a gentle boil until the potato and lentils are cooked.

4. Stir in the yoghurt or cream and taste for seasoning.

5. To serve, ladle into hot bowls and garnish with the parsley.

This light broth can be made with whatever produce is around. I like to use fresh borlotti beans or broad beans when they're in season, and diced heritage tomatoes of differing colours or diced roast beetroot work well, too, and look very pretty.

SPRING VEGETABLE BROTH WITH BUTTERNUT, FENNEL AND MINTED PEA PURÉE **FOR 6**

30 g butter

50 ml extra virgin olive oil

1 large red onion, peeled and thinly sliced

2 cloves garlic, peeled and roughly chopped

2 tsp fresh thyme leaves

2 bay leaves

1 wine glass aromatic white wine (riesling, viognier or pinot gris all work well)

800 ml vegetable stock

300 ml tomato juice (or purée 4 tomatoes and pass through a sieve)

2 carrots, peeled and thinly sliced

1 stalk celery, thinly sliced

1 small head fennel, thinly sliced (avoid the woody base)

100 g peas (fresh or frozen), blanched and refreshed

1 small handful mint leaves

2 spring onions, thinly sliced

¼ tsp lemon zest

2 tbsp lemon juice

salt and freshly ground black pepper

1. Cook the butter over moderate heat until nut-brown, then add half the oil.

2. Add the onion, garlic, thyme and bay leaves and sauté until the onion has softened.

3. Add the wine and boil to reduce by two-thirds, then add the stock and bring to a gentle boil.

4. Add the tomato juice, carrots, celery and fennel and cook for 5 minutes.

5. Meanwhile, mash or roughly blitz the peas with the mint, spring onions and lemon zest and juice. Set aside.

6. Taste soup for seasoning and ladle into bowls. Spoon the minted pea purée on top and drizzle with the remaining oil.

This soup couldn't be simpler or tastier. The turmeric adds a really subtle background earthiness – but it can be replaced with saffron.

TOMATO, RED ONION AND CAPSICUM SOUP WITH FETA CREAM FOR 4

2 red onions, peeled and sliced

3 red capsicums, stems removed,
    deseeded and sliced

3 tbsp extra virgin olive oil

¼ tsp cumin seeds

2 tsp fresh thyme leaves

½ tsp ground turmeric

8 ripe tomatoes, quartered (or 600 g
    tinned chopped tomatoes)

400 ml water

salt and freshly ground black pepper

a little sugar

120 g feta

80 ml cold water

1. Sauté the onions and capsicums over moderate heat in 2 tbsp oil until caramelized.

2. Add the cumin seeds, three-quarters of the thyme and the turmeric and cook for another minute, stirring constantly.

3. Add the tomatoes and the water and bring to a boil. Simmer with a lid on for 20 minutes, then roughly purée either in a blender or with a stick blender.

4. Taste for seasoning (a little sugar might be needed) and put back on the heat to keep warm.

5. While the soup is cooking, purée the feta, the remaining olive oil and the cold water in a small blender (or use a stick blender) until smooth.

6. To serve, ladle the soup into four warm bowls, spoon on the feta cream and sprinkle with the reserved thyme.

This soup is quite rich and filling so you don't need to serve large portions; it makes a great mini soup for a multi-course dinner. You do need to make sure the avocados are fully ripe or the flavour will be lost.

CHILLED AVOCADO AND GINGER SOUP WITH SHRIMP SALAD FOR 4

2 large ripe avocados
50 ml lime or lemon juice
½ green chilli or ½ tsp chilli sauce
  (more or less to taste)
250 ml plain Greek-style yoghurt
4 stems coriander or parsley, shredded
1 tbsp tarragon leaves
4 tbsp avocado oil or olive oil
2 tbsp sushi ginger, finely shredded (or
  fresh ginger, grated)
250 ml ice-cold water
salt
8 radishes, thinly sliced
1 handful shelled cooked shrimps (or
  sliced prawns)

1. Remove the flesh from the avocados, discarding the skin and stone, and place in a blender with the lime or lemon juice, chilli, yoghurt, coriander or parsley, tarragon, half the oil and half the ginger.

2. Add the ice-cold water and blitz to a purée. Season with salt and add a little extra cold water if it seems too thick. You may find it easier to purée this in two batches.

3. Tip into a clean bowl, place plastic wrap on the surface to prevent it discolouring and refrigerate for 1 hour. Place four soup bowls in the fridge as well.

4. To serve, give the soup a whisk and taste for seasoning – it may need a little extra citrus juice or salt. Divide among the four chilled bowls. Scatter on the radishes, shrimps and the remaining ginger, then drizzle on the remaining avocado oil.

This autumnal soup smells really lovely as it arrives at the table – earthy, but with fresh notes from the mint and balsamic.

LENTIL AND PARSNIP SOUP WITH BALSAMIC ONIONS **FOR 4**

4 tbsp olive oil

3 red onions, peeled and thinly sliced

4 tbsp balsamic vinegar

a little caster sugar

2 bay leaves

1 tbsp fresh rosemary leaves, roughly chopped

½ tsp smoked paprika, regular paprika or cayenne pepper

200 g lentils, either green or Puy, rinsed briefly in cold water

800 ml vegetable stock

2 parsnips, peeled and cut into small dice

salt and freshly ground black pepper

1 large handful flat parsley leaves

1 small handful mint leaves

50 g plain yoghurt

1. Heat a medium-sized pot, add two-thirds of the olive oil and sauté the onions until they begin to caramelize. Tip half of them out into a bowl, then add the balsamic vinegar to the pot and cook over a low heat to evaporate it. If the onions taste a little sharp, add a little caster sugar as they cook.

2. Once they're done, tip them into another bowl then return the other onions back to the pot – don't wash it out.

3. Add the bay leaves, rosemary, paprika or cayenne pepper, lentils and stock. Bring to the boil and turn to a simmer.

4. Meanwhile, sit another pan over a high heat and add the remaining oil and the parsnips. Cook over a medium-high heat to colour them, stirring frequently, then add to the lentils. Once the lentils and parsnip are both cooked, taste for seasoning and mix in the parsley and mint.

5. To serve, put the yoghurt into the bottom of four hot bowls and ladle the soup on top, then spoon on the balsamic onions.

This chunky soup could almost be a meal in itself as it's robust, wholesome and very tasty. I love to put chickpeas in it, but you could also make it with cannellini, flageolet or butter beans instead.

PUMPKIN, GINGER, CHICKPEA AND CHEESE SOUP FOR 6–8

1 large white onion, peeled and sliced
1 large leek, rinsed and thinly sliced
2 cloves garlic, peeled and chopped
1 thumb ginger, peeled and chopped
50 g butter
2 good pinches saffron (or ½ tsp turmeric)
600 g pumpkin or butternut squash, peeled, deseeded and roughly chopped
600 ml vegetable stock
1 x 400 g can chickpeas, drained and rinsed well under running water
200 ml cream
coarsely ground black pepper
salt
freshly grated nutmeg, to taste
60 g coarsely grated cheese (try an aged Cheddar or pecorino)
100 ml sour cream, to garnish
chives, to garnish

1. Sauté the onion, leek, garlic and ginger in the butter over a low heat with the lid on, stirring occasionally, until everything softens and wilts.

2. Add the saffron (or turmeric), pumpkin or squash and half the stock, then cook over a low heat with the lid on until the pumpkin or squash is almost cooked. Mash it with a potato masher – it doesn't need to be smooth.

3. Add the drained chickpeas, the remaining stock, the cream and plenty of coarsely ground pepper. Bring to a boil, then reduce to a simmer with the lid on and cook for 15 minutes.

4. Season with salt and add nutmeg to taste. Stir in the cheese and ladle into piping hot bowls. Dollop on the sour cream and snip a few chives over top.

This incredibly simple and refreshing soup may seem like a glorified lassi, but it's surprisingly hearty due to the coconut milk. It's based on a terrific Turkish summer soup where dried yoghurt powder is mixed with water, so if you'd prefer to make it without the coconut milk just use plain yoghurt.

CHILLED CUCUMBER, COCONUT AND DILL SOUP **FOR 6**

2 cucumbers
1 clove garlic, peeled (optional)
600 ml unsweetened coconut milk
100 ml lemon juice (plus a little extra)
salt and freshly ground black pepper
1 heaped tbsp dill, snipped

1. Top and tail the cucumbers and wipe their skins with a damp cloth. Cut a 5 cm piece from one of them, set aside for later, then cut the remaining flesh into thick chunks and place in a blender (not a food processor) with the garlic, coconut milk and lemon juice. Blitz it to a smooth consistency – it may be easier to do this in two batches.

2. Taste for seasoning, then place in the fridge to chill for at least 4 hours. Ideally, leave it overnight for the flavours to develop.

3. An hour before serving, dice the reserved cucumber and mix with ½ tsp salt – leave it to 'cure' for 30 minutes before rinsing and mixing with the dill.

4. To serve, whisk the soup vigorously and adjust seasoning and acidity (add more lemon juice if it needs it), then ladle into chilled bowls and top with the cucumber dill salsa.

This is a delicious soup which is both comforting and somehow light, due to the peas and asparagus. If asparagus isn't around, just make it without increasing the peas to 300 g.

CHUNKY CREAMY PEA, ASPARAGUS AND HAM SOUP
FOR 6-8

1 ham knuckle (hock), weighing about 700 g–1 kg

4 bay leaves

1 bouquet garni (or tie some rosemary, thyme, sage and oregano stalks together)

2 onions, peeled and sliced

200 g asparagus (snap off the tough ends and reserve for the stock)

100 g red lentils (or split peas – although you'll need to soak the latter in warm water for 2 hours and then drain)

1 large potato, peeled and diced

200 g peas (fresh or frozen)

100 ml cream

salt and freshly ground black pepper

1 handful parsley, roughly chopped

1. Place the ham knuckle in a large pot and cover with cold water. Slowly bring to the boil, then drain. Do this once more, and drain it again.

2. Put ham knuckle back in the pot and cover with cold water again. Add the bay leaves, herbs, onions and asparagus ends, then bring to the boil.

3. Lower the heat and simmer for 90 minutes with the lid slightly ajar, removing any foam as it rises.

4. Using a pair of tongs or a large spoon, carefully remove the ham knuckle and place on a plate to cool.

5. Strain 2 litres of the stock into a clean pot and add the lentils and potato. Bring to a rapid simmer, and simmer until they're cooked.

6. Meanwhile, remove the meat from the ham knuckle and chop it roughly or shred it.

7. Cut the asparagus stems into 1 cm lengths.

8. Once the lentils are cooked, add the peas, cream and ham to the pot and simmer for 5 minutes. Stir in the asparagus and cook for just 1 minute.

9. Taste for seasoning, mix in the parsley and serve.

This delicious soup is based loosely on chowder. It's rich because of the coconut milk and sweet corn, but has an earthiness from the mussels. You can use prawns or scallops, if you prefer.

SWEET CORN, MUSSEL, COCONUT AND LEMONGRASS SOUP **FOR 4**

2 onions, peeled and thinly sliced

2 thumbs fresh ginger, peeled and finely chopped or grated

½ red chilli, chopped (more or less to taste)

vegetable oil

1 large potato, peeled and cut into 1 cm dice

1 stem lemongrass, bashed with a rolling pin to bruise, but kept in one piece

1 tsp turmeric (or good pinch saffron)

3 cobs sweet corn, kernels cut off

500 ml unsweetened coconut milk

300 ml fish stock or vegetable stock

1 kg mussels in the shell, scraped of barnacles and beards

salt and freshly ground black pepper

1 handful coriander or parsley or dill, including the stalks, coarsely shredded

1. Sauté the onions, ginger and chilli in a few tablespoons of vegetable oil until beginning to caramelize, stirring frequently.

2. Mix in the potato, lemongrass and turmeric (or saffron), put a lid on the pot and cook over low heat for 5 minutes, stirring occasionally.

3. Add the sweet corn kernels, coconut milk and stock. Bring to the boil, then reduce to a gentle boil and cook until the potato is done.

4. You can keep the soup chunky or purée it – it's up to you. Just be sure to remove the lemongrass before puréeing it.

5. Meanwhile, put the mussels in another pot with a few tablespoons of water. Put the lid on and cook over a high heat. Check after 3 minutes, and remove any that have opened and reserve. Discard any that haven't opened after 5 minutes. Strain the cooking liquid, taste that it's pleasant and add to the soup. If it tastes too salty, add just enough to season the soup.

6. Once they're cool enough to handle, remove the mussels from their shells.

7. Bring the soup back to a simmer, then stir in the mussels and taste for seasoning. Ladle the soup into very hot bowls and scatter with the herbs.

This classic Greek soup contains chicken and egg and is both light and rich at the same time. It's enriched with eggs, but lightened with lemon juice. Sounds odd, but it works really well.

AVGOLEMONO SOUP **FOR 4**

oil, for cooking
2 skinless chicken breasts (chicken thighs and legs are also good here)
1 litre chicken stock
90 g long grain rice, rinsed briefly in a sieve under cold water
2 egg whites
4 egg yolks
4 tbsp lemon juice (or more to taste)
salt and freshly ground black pepper
extra virgin olive oil and snipped chives, to garnish

1. Heat a pot with a little oil and add the chicken breasts. Seal on both sides without colouring too much, add the chicken stock and bring to the boil. Turn to a simmer, put a lid on and cook for 5 minutes. Turn the breasts over and cook until they're done.

2. Take chicken from the stock and leave until cool enough to handle, then shred or dice. Skim any excess fat from the surface of the stock and bring it back to a simmer.

3. Add the rice to the stock and simmer until just cooked – around 12–15 minutes.

4. Once the rice is ready, whisk the egg whites for 10 seconds until foamy, then whisk in the yolks and then the lemon juice. Ladle half a cup of the simmering broth into the egg mixture, whisking as you do, then quickly pour this back into the simmering broth. Stir continuously with a spoon and cook over a low heat until the soup comes to a simmer. Do not allow it to boil or the egg will curdle, but it is important that you cook it until it has thickened a little, much like a thin custard.

5. Take off the heat, stir in the chicken and taste for seasoning.

6. To serve, ladle into warm bowls, drizzle with the olive oil and sprinkle a few chives on top.

This semi-chunky soup is simple to make and very tasty. You can make it from a variety of mushrooms or just plain old field mushrooms, but button mushrooms by themselves won't have enough flavour. Walnuts work just as well as hazelnuts.

CREAMY MUSHROOM AND HAZELNUT SOUP FOR 4

30 g butter
1 leek, rinsed and thinly sliced
2 cloves garlic, peeled and sliced
20 sage leaves
500 g mushrooms, sliced
100 g roasted, skinless hazelnuts,
    roughly chopped
600 ml vegetable stock
2 tbsp soy sauce
200 ml cream
salt (or extra soy sauce)
50 ml crème fraîche, to garnish
1 tbsp snipped chives, to garnish

1. Cook the butter in a wide pan until it becomes nut-brown in colour.

2. Add the leek, garlic and sage and sauté over moderate heat until the leek has completely wilted, stirring frequently.

3. Add the mushrooms and hazelnuts and cook until the mushrooms wilt.

4. Stir in the stock, soy sauce and cream and bring to a boil. Turn the heat to a rapid simmer, put a lid on and cook for 15 minutes.

5. Use a stick blender to partially purée the soup, leaving it semi-chunky – although you can keep it fully chunky if you prefer. If using a 'bar blender', blend small amounts at a time so the hot soup doesn't burn you.

6. Bring back to a simmer and taste for seasoning, adding salt or extra soy, if needed.

7. To serve, ladle into hot bowls and garnish with crème fraîche and chives.

Pumpkin soup is the one thing that every New Zealander can make – or at least that's how it was in my day. This version is chunky and hearty, which makes it a perfect winter's lunch.

CURRIED PUMPKIN, LENTIL AND TOMATO SOUP **FOR 6**

80 g butter
2 onions, peeled and thinly sliced
½ tsp cumin seeds
500 g pumpkin, peeled and diced
2 tsp curry powder
100 g lentils, either green or Puy, rinsed briefly in cold water
300 ml tomato passata
2 bay leaves
1 litre vegetable stock
200 ml cream or plain yoghurt
salt and freshly ground black pepper

1. In a large pot, heat the butter until it turns nut-brown in colour.

2. Add the onion and cumin seeds and cook over moderate heat to caramelize the onion, stirring often.

3. Add the pumpkin and curry powder and cook for 2 minutes, stirring frequently.

4. Add the lentils, passata, bay leaves and stock and bring to the boil.

5. Simmer with a lid on the pot until both the pumpkin and lentils are cooked, around 30 minutes, skimming off any foam that rises to the surface.

6. Once it's done, stir in the cream or yoghurt and cook for another few minutes. Taste for seasoning and serve piping hot.

Lovely served hot in winter or chilled in summer, this soup takes its inspiration from
Spain and is great when accompanied by a glass of chilled Fino *sherry.*

TOMATO AND PIQUILLO PEPPER SOUP WITH YOGHURT AND CROUTONS **FOR 4**

1 large red onion, peeled and thinly
  sliced
3 tbsp extra virgin olive oil
3 cloves garlic, peeled and sliced
1 tbsp fresh thyme leaves
½ tsp cumin seeds
3 tbsp sherry vinegar or good red wine
  vinegar
600 g tinned peeled tomatoes
250 g tinned Spanish piquillo peppers
  (or tinned red capsicums and 1 tsp
  smoked paprika)
250 ml water
2 slices one-day-old bread (slightly
  stale)
salt
4 tbsp runny yoghurt

1. Preheat oven to 170°C.

2. Sauté the onion in 2 tbsp olive oil until it wilts, then add the garlic, thyme and cumin seeds and continue to cook until caramelized.

3. Stir in the vinegar and cook until it has almost evaporated.

4. Add the tomatoes, peppers and water, and bring to the boil. Reduce to a simmer, and cook for 15 minutes, stirring occasionally.

5. Cut the bread into small cubes and toss with the remaining oil and a little salt, then bake until golden; around 10–15 minutes.

6. Purée the soup very finely and pass through a sieve if necessary.

7. To serve, ladle the soup (either gently reheated or served very chilled) into bowls, drizzle on the yoghurt and sprinkle with the croutons.

Gazpacho is probably the world's best-known cold soup – there are many variations and this is one of them. It may seem quite fiddly but bear with me – it's terrific. If you can, make the soup the day before you want it.

CHILLED TOMATO BROTH WITH CROUTONS AND MINT **FOR 4-6**

10 large ripe tomatoes
150 ml cider vinegar or white vinegar
50 g caster sugar
4 cloves garlic, peeled and sliced
1 tbsp mustard seeds
1 tbsp fresh thyme leaves
3 tbsp olive oil
salt and freshly ground black pepper
2 slices stale bread, crusts removed, cut
  into cubes
12 mint leaves
1 hard-boiled egg, peeled and chopped

1. Bring a pot of water to the boil and have a bowl of iced water ready. Cut a shallow X into the base of the tomatoes. Drop 5 tomatoes into the water and after 20 seconds remove them and place in the iced water. Do the same to the remainder.

2. After a few minutes peel the tomatoes, reserving the peel. Place the peel in a saucepan with the vinegar, sugar, garlic, mustard seeds and thyme. Cut the tomatoes into quarters and use a teaspoon to scoop out the seeds, add the seeds and juice to the pan. Bring the mixture to the boil, then simmer for 15 minutes and leave to cool.

3. Dice 4 of the deseeded tomato quarters, mix with 1 tbsp oil and place in the fridge.

4. Once the tomato vinegar liquid has cooled place it in a blender (not a food processor) and blitz it to a fine purée, then pass through a sieve and discard the pulp.

5. Rinse out the blender and add the remaining tomato quarters and the tomato vinegar liquid. Purée until smooth – you might want to do this in two batches. Season and place in the fridge to chill or, ideally, overnight.

6. In a frying pan, sauté the cubes of bread in the remaining oil until golden and crisp.

7. Shred the mint and mix with the diced tomatoes in the fridge. Chop or coarsely grate the boiled egg.

8. To serve, give the soup a good stir and taste for seasoning, then ladle into chilled bowls. Scatter with the croutons, boiled egg and minted tomato.

This soup was originally intended to be served hot, but I realized it was delicious chilled (actually, it's good either way). The salty feta brings all the flavours together, a mixture of sweet and savoury. If you don't have miso paste, use soy sauce and add a little more seasoning.

CHILLED BUTTERNUT, MISO AND CHILLI SOUP WITH FETA **FOR 6-8**

6 shallots or 2 onions, peeled and sliced

3 cloves garlic, peeled and sliced

3 tbsp olive oil

500 g butternut squash or pumpkin, skin and seeds removed, sliced 1 cm thick

1 tsp dried oregano leaves (or slightly more fresh leaves)

1–2 tsp dried chilli flakes (more or less to taste)

2 tbsp runny light honey

700 ml vegetable stock (you may need extra to thin the soup)

3 tbsp miso paste

salt and freshly ground black pepper

100 g feta, crumbled into chunks

1 spring onion, thinly sliced

1. Sauté the shallots or onions and garlic in the oil until just beginning to caramelize – you don't want them too coloured.

2. Add the squash or pumpkin, oregano and chilli flakes, and cook for another 4 minutes, stirring often. Add the honey and vegetable stock and bring to the boil. Put a lid on the pot and simmer rapidly until the butternut is cooked.

3. Stir in the miso and simmer another 3 minutes, then remove from the heat and leave to cool. Purée quite finely and taste for seasoning. Place in a container and chill in the fridge for at least 8 hours.

4. To serve, stir the soup and taste for seasoning. If it's too thick, whisk in some extra chilled vegetable stock. Ladle into chilled bowls and garnish with the feta and spring onion.

This decadent soup is inspired by San Francisco's famous Trader Vic's 'Bongo Bongo Soup' that a friend cooked for me in New Zealand in the mid 1980s. It's packed with oysters – oyster lovers may feel it's sacrilegious to cook them but it's worth it, and even frozen oysters work well. The soup can be made with either coconut milk or cream, each lending a different feel to the finished soup.

OYSTER, COCONUT AND SPINACH SOUP **FOR 4-6**

100 g shallots, peeled and thinly sliced (2–3 banana shallots or 6 regular shallots)

50 g butter

200 ml fish stock

600 ml coconut cream (or cream)

1 large potato, peeled and coarsely grated

2 spring onions, cut into 1 cm pieces

300 g spinach, thick stems removed, leaves washed and coarsely shredded

12 oysters from the shell (you can use up to 24)

salt and freshly ground black pepper

2 tbsp desiccated coconut, lightly toasted

1. Sauté the shallots in the butter over moderate heat, making sure not to colour them.

2. Add the fish stock, coconut milk and grated potato and bring to the boil, then add the spring onions and cook on a rapid simmer for 4 minutes.

3. Stir in the spinach leaves and cook for another 3 minutes.

4. Stir in the oysters and cook for another 2 minutes.

5. Blend until smooth (a stick blender is easiest), then bring back to a gentle simmer and taste for seasoning.

6. To serve, ladle into warmed bowls and sprinkle with the toasted coconut.

This Japanese-inspired broth is both sweetish and savoury, and deceptively hearty.
If you don't have swede, use parsnips, celeriac or pumpkin, or a combination of all of
them. Kombu seaweed, mirin and miso are available at Japanese food stores and some
health food shops.

CHUNKY SWEDE, MISO, LEEK AND CARROT BROTH **FOR 4-6**

1 leek, rinsed and thinly sliced

1 thumb ginger, peeled and grated

2 tbsp sesame oil or vegetable oil

400 g swede, peeled and cut into 1 cm chunks

2 carrots, peeled and thinly sliced

1 x 8 cm piece kombu seaweed, briefly rinsed to remove surface whiteness then patted dry with kitchen paper

50 ml mirin or runny honey

700 ml hot water

2 tbsp white miso paste (shiro miso)

3 tbsp soy sauce

salt (or extra soy sauce)

1. Sauté the leek and ginger in the oil over moderate heat, stirring often, until the leek wilts. Don't allow it to colour.

2. Stir in the swede, carrots, kombu, mirin or honey and the hot water. Bring to a rapid simmer, then cook with a lid on for 5 minutes.

3. Add 600 ml hot water, bring to a gentle boil, then simmer with the lid on until the swede is cooked.

4. Mix the miso and soy sauce with 100 ml hot water, then stir into the broth.

5. Bring back to a rapid simmer and cook uncovered for 5 minutes.

6. Taste for seasoning, adding extra soy or salt as needed.

7. To serve, remove the kombu and ladle the broth into preheated bowls.

| CHAPTER THREE |

PASTA, RICE AND NOODLES

The addition of soy sauce to risotto is completely unorthodox, but it makes it really tasty.
I love sage with butternut squash, but thyme, oregano and rosemary also work well.

BUTTERNUT SQUASH AND LEEK RISOTTO **FOR 4–6 AS A LIGHT MAIN COURSE**

60 g butter
1 handful sage leaves, torn
500 g diced, peeled butternut squash or
   pumpkin
2 litres light vegetable or chicken stock
1 leek, rinsed and sliced
2 bay leaves
350 g risotto rice
salt
4 tbsp soy sauce, plus extra for
   seasoning
50 g Parmesan, grated
100 g mascarpone (optional)

1. Cook half the butter until it turns golden brown. Add the sage leaves and cook until they wilt, then add the squash or pumpkin and cook over a moderate heat for a minute, stirring frequently to coat the squash with butter.

2. Add 250 ml of the stock and cook over a high heat with a lid on until the squash is almost cooked through, stirring occasionally. Once it's ready, mash about a quarter of it in the pot and keep warm. Bring the rest of the stock to a simmer.

3. Meanwhile, in a larger pot heat up the remaining butter and when it begins to sizzle add the leek and bay leaves and cook until the leek has completely softened. Add rice and a little salt and cook over medium-high heat for 1 minute, stirring constantly.

4. Stir in enough stock to cover the rice by 2 cm, then turn the heat down to a rapid simmer. Leave it to gently cook until most of the liquid is absorbed. Stir in another 250 ml of stock, then leave until it is nearly absorbed. The rice must be covered with stock at all times – even if just by a few millimetres.

5. Keep cooking this way and after 12 minutes the rice should be al dente, softening on the outside and a little firm in the centre. At this point, stir in the squash mixture and soy sauce and continue cooking until the rice is just cooked.

6. Put a lid on the pot, turn the heat off and leave to rest for a couple of minutes.

7. Stir in the Parmesan and mascarpone (if using) and taste for seasoning, adding extra soy or salt to taste, and serve immediately.

Because it's fairly simple, this dish is best served as a starter. If you want to serve it as a main course, you'll need to add more to it, like chopped blanched broccoli and green beans, diced smoked chicken or prawns.

LINGUINE WITH MINTED PISTACHIO PESTO **FOR 6 STARTERS**

150 g pistachios, unsalted and shelled,
  lightly toasted
1 handful mint leaves
1 handful parsley leaves
2 cloves garlic, peeled
salt and freshly ground black pepper
150 ml extra virgin olive oil
100 g Parmesan, finely grated
400 g linguine

1. Reserve 2 tbsp of the nuts, then put the remainder in a food processor with the mint, parsley and garlic. Blitz for 10 seconds, then scrape down the bowl.

2. Add a little salt and half the oil, then blitz for 5 seconds.

3. Add about two-thirds of the cheese and the remaining oil and blitz for another 5 seconds. Pour into a large warm bowl and taste for seasoning.

4. Cook the linguine in lightly salted water until al dente.

5. Take 50 ml (just over 3 tbsp) of the cooking water and add it to the pesto.

6. Drain the pasta in a colander and add to the pesto. Toss it all together thoroughly and taste for seasoning.

7. Serve in warmed bowls with the remaining Parmesan and pistachios sprinkled on top.

A big dish of this bubbling away in the oven is very comforting. I like to make it with a combination of minced meats, including lamb, beef and pork, but this version is a lot simpler shopping-wise. If you can't find cannelloni tubes, layer the mince between lasagne sheets and it'll still be delicious.

PORK AND MUSHROOM CANNELLONI
FOR 6 MAIN COURSES

2 large onions, peeled and diced

4 cloves garlic, peeled and chopped

80 g butter, plus more for the baking dish

400 g coarse lean pork mince

1 tsp each chopped fresh rosemary, sage and thyme

¼ tsp grated nutmeg

250 g mushrooms, sliced (portobello, chestnut or button)

1 tsp tomato paste

250 ml red or white wine (don't use anything too sweet)

salt and freshly ground black pepper

18 cannelloni tubes

1 x 400 g tin chopped tomatoes (or use fresh ones, chopped)

200 ml crème fraîche

50 g Parmesan, grated

1. Preheat oven to 180°C. You need a deep-ish baking dish that will be able to hold all the cannelloni tubes in one layer. Butter it heavily.

2. Sauté the onions and garlic in the butter until the onions have wilted.

3. Add the mince and herbs and cook for a few minutes, mashing the mince down with a spoon to break it up.

4. Add the nutmeg, mushrooms, tomato paste and wine. Stir well and bring to a simmer. Put a lid on and cook for 30 minutes.

5. Take the lid off and cook until most of the liquid has evaporated. Taste for seasoning and take off the heat.

6. Once it's cool enough to handle, fill the cannelloni tubes with the mixture, using either a teaspoon or a piping bag without a nozzle. Lay them snugly in the baking dish.

7. Mix the tomatoes and crème fraîche together in a small pan and bring to the boil. Pour over the cannelloni and sprinkle with Parmesan, then bake in the middle of the oven until the sauce is bubbling and the top is golden; around 30–40 minutes.

Whilst the Italians are famous for their risotto, the Spanish are also huge growers and consumers of rice. Whether it be rabbit and snail paella on the mainland or squid ink-infused black rice from the Canary Islands, Calasparra rice is number one in Spain.

'SPANISH RICE' WITH CHORIZO, MANCHEGO, ALMONDS AND FIGS

FOR 6–8 STARTERS

1 tbsp butter

250 g cooking chorizo, cut into smallish cubes

1 large onion, peeled and thinly sliced

3 tbsp extra virgin olive oil

400 g Calasparra or short-grain rice

1 tsp coarse sea salt

1.8 litres chicken or vegetable stock, at simmering point

8 dried figs, hard stem removed, thinly sliced

80 g Manchego or Parmesan, grated

salt and freshly ground black pepper

60 g salted almonds, roughly chopped

1. Cook the butter in a medium pot until nut-brown. Add the chorizo and cook over a moderate heat for a few minutes, stirring frequently.

2. Add the onion and 1 tbsp oil and cook until the onion is caramelized. Stir it often as it tends to stick to the pan.

3. Spoon the chorizo-onion mixture into a bowl and place the pot back on the heat – don't wipe it out unless you have some burnt bits on the bottom.

4. Add the remaining oil to the pan along with the rice and coarse sea salt (use less if it's fine salt). Cook over high heat for 2 minutes, stirring continuously, to colour the rice.

5. Pour in 500 ml (2 cups) stock and turn the heat to a simmer – it will bubble furiously at first so stand back. Once it's at a simmer and the stock has been absorbed, add another 250 ml – a ladle is the easiest way to do this. Keep cooking like this until the last ladleful of stock is left – the mixture should be a little like runny porridge with a little bite to the rice; if it's soft or mushy, don't add any more stock.

6. Place the chorizo and figs in the pan with the last of the stock, stir in three-quarters of the cheese and taste for seasoning. Put a lid on the pot, turn the heat off and leave to rest for a few minutes.

7. To serve, mix it all together then spoon into bowls, sprinkling the almonds and remaining cheese on top.

I used golden beets in this recipe because I love their colour and taste, but you can substitute them with red or other coloured beets if you prefer. The pesto is great dolloped onto chicken or fish or tossed through steamed broccoli.

FARFALLE WITH GOLDEN BEETROOT PESTO, PEAS AND MINT **FOR 4 LUNCHES OR 6 STARTERS**

3 golden beetroot (about 300 g)
100 g macadamia nuts, almonds or pine
   nuts, lightly toasted
2 cloves garlic, peeled
1 handful coriander leaves and stalks,
   shredded
1 large handful basil leaves
1 handful flat parsley leaves
80 ml extra virgin olive oil (plus 3 tbsp
   extra, for finishing)
40 g Parmesan, grated
salt and freshly ground black pepper
400 g dried farfalle or fusilli
200 g peas (fresh or frozen)
1 handful mint leaves, torn

1. Preheat oven to 200°C.

2. Wash any dirt from the beetroot, then wrap them tightly in foil, place on a baking tray and roast for 45–90 minutes. They're cooked when you can poke a skewer or thin, sharp knife through the foil with little resistance.

3. Leave them to cool for 10 minutes before rubbing their skins off with your fingers or a sharp knife. Wear gloves if you're worried about your hands being stained. Dice them all.

4. Place the nuts and garlic in a food processor and blitz to give coarse crumbs. Add one-third of the beetroot, the coriander, basil and parsley and blitz for 10 seconds. Scrape down the sides, add the olive oil and blitz again to make a coarse paste. Tip into a bowl and stir in the Parmesan. If the mixture looks too dry, stir in a little extra olive oil. Taste for seasoning, adding salt and pepper if needed.

5. Boil the pasta in plenty of lightly salted water until al dente. Add the peas, bring back to the boil and cook for another minute before draining in a colander.

6. Tip pasta and peas into a large warm bowl, add the diced beetroot, 3 tbsp extra virgin olive oil, the mint and the pesto, and salt to taste.

7. Toss it all together and divide among four warmed bowls. You can offer extra grated Parmesan on the side, if you like.

The combination of chickpeas and pasta makes this dish really comforting, but the addition of the chilli and basil gives it a lovely 'oomph' as well. It's quite rich, so I prefer to serve it as a starter rather than a main course.

FETTUCCINE WITH CHILLI, BASIL AND CHICKPEAS **FOR 4-6 STARTERS**

400 g fettuccine

4 tbsp extra virgin olive oil

½–1 tsp crushed red chilli flakes or 1 red or green chilli, finely chopped

2 cloves garlic, peeled and roughly chopped

200 g drained, cooked chickpeas (canned ones, rinsed well, are fine to use)

1 large handful basil leaves, torn

100 g Parmesan, finely grated

1. Bring a large pot of lightly salted water to the boil and cook the fettuccine until almost cooked – it needs to be a little underdone. Reserve 150 ml of the cooking water, then drain the pasta in a colander.

2. While the pasta is cooking, heat up a pot and add the oil, chilli and garlic. Cook over a moderate heat until the garlic turns golden – stir frequently to stop it burning and sticking.

3. Add the drained chickpeas and cook for another 2 minutes, stirring frequently.

4. Add the drained pasta and the reserved cooking water and mix it in well. Put a lid on the pot and cook for 3–4 minutes until the pasta is fully cooked, stirring occasionally to prevent it sticking to the pan.

5. Mix the basil and half the Parmesan into the pasta, then divide among four warmed bowls. Sprinkle with the remaining Parmesan as you serve it.

This sauce is actually very simple to make, but it will only work if the tomatoes and capsicums are ripe and sweet. I like to serve this as a first course as it's quite light, but you can serve it as a main course for four, adding some fried chorizo or smoked fish to bulk it up.

TOMATO AND CAPSICUM SPAGHETTI

FOR 8 STARTERS

3 capsicums (use a mixture of red, yellow and orange if you can)
6 tomatoes, peeled
4 cloves garlic, peeled and chopped
2 bay leaves, torn into pieces
3 tbsp orange or lemon juice
6 tbsp olive oil
1 tsp chilli flakes (more or less to taste)
1 small handful soft herbs (tarragon, basil, mint, parsley – a mixture or just one or two)
salt and freshly ground black pepper
400 g dried spaghetti
100 g Parmesan, grated

1. Grill or barbecue the capsicums until their skins blacken. Put in a plastic bag and leave to cool. Remove stalks and peel, cut in half and remove seeds, then cut into strips.

2. Cut the tomatoes in half crossways and scoop out seeds. Reserve the seeds. Cut the tomatoes into wedges.

3. Put the seeds in a small pot with the garlic, bay leaves, orange or lemon juice and half the olive oil. Bring to a boil, then rapidly simmer for 10 minutes. Pass through a fine sieve into a clean pan, squeezing out as much juice as you can. Add the chilli flakes, the remaining olive oil, the grilled capsicums and the tomato wedges.

4. Bring to a bubble and cook over a rapid simmer for 5 minutes, then stir in the herbs and taste for seasoning.

5. Cook the spaghetti in lightly salted water until al dente, then drain in a colander.

6. Toss the spaghetti with the tomato sauce and serve in warm bowls, topped with the Parmesan.

Use any long pasta for this, such as linguine, although, to be honest, it would work with any shape you like. The trick is to add the broccoli to the cooking pasta before it's fully cooked, which is fairly easy to judge.

PRAWN, CAPSICUM, BROCCOLI AND HAZELNUT PASTA WITH OLIVE SALSA **FOR 4 MAIN COURSES**

200 g pitted olives, roughly chopped

1 small handful mint leaves, shredded

2 spring onions, thinly sliced

4 tbsp extra virgin olive oil

1 large red onion, peeled and thinly sliced

4 cloves garlic, peeled and chopped

a few pinches cayenne pepper, paprika or smoked paprika

2 red capsicums, deseeded and sliced

2 tbsp lemon juice

500 g large raw prawn tails, peeled

4 tbsp roasted hazelnuts, peeled and finely chopped

salt and freshly ground black pepper

400 g dried pasta

1 medium head broccoli, cut into florets

1. Mix the olives with the mint and spring onions and 2 tbsp olive oil. Reserve.

2. Sauté the onion in the remaining oil until caramelized. Add the garlic, cayenne or paprika and capsicums and cook until they have softened.

3. Add the lemon juice and cook until it evaporates.

4. Add the prawns and half the hazelnuts and cook over moderate heat, stirring, until the prawns are almost cooked through, then turn the heat off and keep warm. They'll continue to cook, so keep them a little underdone. Taste for seasoning.

5. Cook the pasta in plenty of lightly salted boiling water until almost al dente. Add the broccoli and continue to cook until they're both done.

6. Drain in a colander, then mix with the prawns.

7. Divide between four bowls, sprinkle with the reserved hazelnuts, then spoon on the olive salsa.

Udon noodles can be found at any Japanese food store. They're mostly dried but sometimes come pre-cooked in a tightly sealed bag; the latter take much less cooking. If you can't find them, use spaghetti or linguine instead.

MUSSEL, CHORIZO AND EGGPLANT UDON NOODLES **FOR 4 MAIN COURSES OR 6 STARTERS**

1 kg mussels (the ones in the photo are lovely green-lipped mussels from New Zealand)

1 red onion, peeled and sliced

2 tbsp olive oil

300 g cooking chorizo, peeled and sliced ½ cm thick

4 cloves garlic, peeled and sliced

1 eggplant, stem removed, cut into 2 cm dice

4 tomatoes, diced

300 g dried udon noodles, or 400 g pre-cooked

salt and freshly ground black pepper

1 handful picked parsley leaves

1. First prepare the mussels. Discard any that are open or have damaged shells. Pull the beards off the rest, then wash thoroughly in plenty of cold water. Place in a pot with 100 ml water, put the lid on and cook over high heat for 5 minutes. Shake the pot from time to time to help the mussels open.

2. At this point most of the mussels will have opened. Remove those ones to a colander sitting in a bowl. Cook the rest for another 2 minutes, then take off the heat. Discard any that haven't opened and tip the rest into the colander. Once they're cool enough to handle, remove half the mussels from their shells and put to one side. Strain the juices through a fine sieve and taste – if very salty, use less in the sauce.

3. Sauté the onion in the olive oil until it begins to caramelize. Add the chorizo, garlic and eggplant and cook over moderate heat for 2 minutes, stirring constantly, until the eggplant begins to colour.

4. Add the tomatoes and 200 ml of the mussel cooking juice (less if the juice is salty) and bring to a simmer, then cook for 10 minutes.

5. Bring a pot of lightly salted water to the boil and drop the noodles in. Bring the water back to a gentle boil and cook until al dente; around 12–15 minutes. If using pre-cooked noodles, boil for 1–2 minutes until heated through, then drain.

6. Add the noodles to the chorizo stew along with the mussels both in and out of their shells. Simmer for 1 minute and taste for seasoning.

7. Divide among four large bowls and sprinkle on the parsley.

I find this dish works well as either a main course or, served slightly smaller, a starter, although I've even served it as a side to a roast leg of lamb with a minted pesto. Any shell or macaroni-type pasta works here as their hollows fill up with the roasting juices and oils.

PUMPKIN, BEAN, GOAT'S CHEESE AND ALMOND PASTA **FOR 4 MAIN COURSES**

500 g pumpkin or butternut squash, peeled, deseeded and cut into 2 cm chunks

2 cloves garlic, peeled and sliced

1 red onion, peeled and thinly sliced

1 tbsp fresh thyme (or any other hard herb)

3 tbsp extra virgin olive oil

freshly ground black pepper

sea salt

hot water

150 g goat's cheese, feta or mozzarella, broken into chunks

100 g flaked almonds, lightly toasted

300 g dried pasta

2 handfuls green beans, ends trimmed, cut into 2 cm lengths

1. Preheat oven to 200°C. Line a roasting dish with baking paper.

2. Put the pumpkin or squash, garlic, red onion, thyme and olive oil in the roasting dish. Season well with lots of pepper and sea salt and mix together. Add a few tablespoons of hot water, then roast until the pumpkin is cooked and coloured, stirring occasionally. It will take 30–40 minutes.

3. Once cooked, sprinkle the cheese and almonds on top and turn the oven off. This stops it cooking any further, but keeps it warm.

4. Cook the pasta in plenty of salted boiling water until al dente. Add the beans to the cooking pasta 2 minutes before it's done. Drain in a colander and tip into a large bowl. Add the pumpkin mixture and any juices in the roasting dish and toss together.

On a warm day, a pasta salad is really good to eat and it usually travels well on a picnic. I like to make this using both red and yellow cherry tomatoes. Any short pasta works well: penne, fusilli, wheels or whatever takes your fancy.

PASTA SALAD WITH CHERRY TOMATOES, CUCUMBER, FETA AND PINE NUTS **FOR 4 MAIN COURSES**

400 g pasta
1 cucumber, peeled
1 tsp flaky salt
300 g cherry tomatoes
100 g pine nuts, toasted
4 tbsp extra virgin olive oil
1 handful parsley leaves
1 handful basil leaves, torn
100 g feta, coarsely grated or crumbled
salt and freshly ground black pepper

1. Cook the pasta in a pot of lightly salted boiling water, then drain.

2. Thinly slice the cucumber and toss with the flaky salt. Leave to sit for 20 minutes, then drain in a colander and run a few cups of cold water over it. Pat dry between kitchen paper and put in a bowl.

3. Cut half the cherry tomatoes in half and add to the cucumber with the pine nuts.

4. Put a frying pan over high heat and add 1 tbsp olive oil and the remaining tomatoes. Cook until the tomatoes begin to pop their skins and colour, then tip onto the cucumber mixture with the rest of the olive oil. Toss it all together, then leave to cool.

5. Mix in the herbs and cheese, and then the pasta. Season well and leave for 20 minutes before serving.

I'm not the greatest fan of Brussels sprouts, but cooked briefly like this they retain a
lovely texture and freshness. Cook the vegetables in a wok or a wide pan over high heat.
Any pasta will work here.

PASTA WITH BROCCOLINI AND BRUSSELS SPROUTS **FOR 4 MAIN COURSES**

400 g dried pasta
½ chilli, chopped (more or less to taste)
4 cloves garlic, peeled and chopped
1 tbsp fresh oregano leaves (or 1 tsp
   dried oregano)
2 tbsp olive oil
150 g Brussels sprouts, trimmed and
   thinly sliced into rings
300 g broccolini, cut into 1 cm pieces
50 g butter, at room temperature
freshly ground black pepper
100 g Parmesan or firm pecorino, grated

1. Cook the pasta in a pot of lightly salted boiling water.

2. While it's cooking, fry the chilli, garlic and oregano in the oil until the garlic begins to colour.

3. Add the Brussels sprouts and cook until they wilt, stirring continuously.

4. Add ½ cup of water from the pasta pot, then turn the heat off.

5. Once the pasta is almost cooked add the broccolini and boil for another minute. Drain in a colander, then tip into a warm bowl.

6. Mix in the butter and plenty of pepper, then mix in the sprouts.

7. Serve in warmed bowls and sprinkle with the Parmesan or pecorino.

Aromatic and very tasty, this rice dish is great to serve alongside slow-roasted shoulder or leg of lamb, roast chicken or as part of a vegetarian buffet. The greater the variety of seeds and nuts you use, the more intriguing the finished dish.

CURRIED NUT, FRUIT AND ORANGE PILAF **FOR 6 AS A SIDE DISH**

40 g butter

1 red onion, peeled and diced

1 tsp curry powder (more or less to taste)

¼ tsp cumin seeds

1 tsp mustard seeds (yellow or black)

50 g mixed dried fruit (apricots, currants, dates), chopped to a similar size

100 g mixed nuts (almonds, cashews, pistachios), toasted and roughly chopped

30 g pumpkin or sunflower seeds

200 g basmati rice, rinsed and drained

2 strips orange peel (make sure there's no bitter white pith)

salt and freshly ground black pepper

600 ml hot water

1. Place a 2-litre pan over moderate heat, add the butter and cook until it turns nut-brown.

2. Add the onion and sauté, stirring frequently, until it softens; about 2 minutes.

3. Add the curry powder, cumin and mustard seeds, dried fruit, nuts and seeds. Fry for 2 minutes, stirring constantly, until the fruit begins to swell.

4. Add the rice, orange peel and ¾ tsp salt and fry for another minute, stirring constantly. Pour on the hot water and bring to the boil.

5. Place a lid on the pot and turn to a simmer. Cook for 10 minutes. Turn the heat off and leave it to sit for 12 minutes. Give it another stir, taste for seasoning and it's ready.

Part of the appeal of this dish is the crispy skin – so it's important you use salmon (or trout) with the skin still on and the scales intact. It may seem that it won't taste great, but it will.

SEARED SALMON ON MUSHROOM AND RICE NOODLE STIR-FRY **FOR 2 MAIN COURSES**

100 g dried rice noodles, any shape you like

boiling water, to cover

2 tbsp olive oil

300 g salmon fillet, bones removed, cut into 4 pieces

1 small leek, rinsed and sliced

1 carrot, peeled and thinly sliced

½ chilli, sliced

120 g Asian mushrooms (shiitake, oyster or shimeji)

1 handful mangetout (snow peas), cut on the diagonal into 3 pieces

3 tbsp soy sauce

1. Put the noodles into a heatproof bowl and pour on enough boiling water to cover – leave to soak for at least 15 minutes.

2. Meanwhile, place a deep frying pan over moderate heat and add 1 tbsp oil.

3. Sit the fish in, skin-side down, and cook over a moderate-high heat for 4 minutes. By this time the skin should have become crispy, but not burnt.

4. Flip the fillets over and cook for just 10 seconds, then remove to a warm plate. Pull the skin off and reserve it.

5. Wipe the pan out with a paper towel (there's no need to wash it). Add another tbsp oil, the leek and carrot and cook over a moderate heat until the vegetables begin to colour, stirring frequently.

6. Add the chilli and mushrooms and cook for another minute, stirring as it cooks.

7. Drain the noodles in a colander and add these to the pan along with the mangetout and soy sauce. Cook for 1–2 minutes over high heat, tossing it all together to warm through.

8. Divide the noodle mixture between two warmed bowls, then flake the salmon on top. Tear the crisp skin into pieces and poke this in as well.

This dish can be made with any short pasta (penne, farfalle, rigatoni, etc.), any minced meat (beef, lamb, pork, venison), any type of canned beans or chickpeas and any firm cheese (Cheddar, Emmental, Gruyère, etc.). It's a meal on its own but even better served with a green salad or steamed green veggies.

BAKED PASTA WITH MEATBALLS AND CHEESE **FOR 4-6 MAIN COURSES**

600 g minced lean meat
3 tbsp Worcestershire sauce or similarly
  spiced sauce or chilli sauce
salt and pepper
200 g dried pasta
1 large onion, peeled and sliced
6 cloves garlic, peeled and sliced
3 tbsp olive oil or butter
1 tbsp chopped fresh mixed herbs
  (rosemary, sage, thyme, oregano) or
  1 tsp dried herbs
1 kg chopped peeled tomatoes, fresh or
  canned
1 x 400 g tin beans, drained
150 g cheese, sliced or grated
¼ cup coarse breadcrumbs

1. Preheat oven to 170°C.

2. Mix the mince with the sauce and a little salt and pepper and roll into 12 even-sized balls.

3. Boil the pasta in lightly salted water for half the time recommended on the packet, then drain in a colander and rinse with cold water.

4. Sauté the onion and garlic in 2 tbsp oil or butter until caramelized, stirring frequently.

5. Stir in the herbs, tomatoes and beans and bring to the boil. Taste and season, then stir in the drained pasta and mix well.

6. Brush a 2½–3 litre baking dish with the remaining oil or butter and spoon in two-thirds of the pasta mixture.

7. Sit the meatballs on top, then cover with the remaining pasta. Lay a sheet of baking paper on top of the pasta and seal with foil or cover with a lid. Bake for 30 minutes in a roasting tray, which will help keep your oven clean.

8. Uncover the dish, scatter with the cheese and breadcrumbs and bake for another 20 minutes until the sauce is bubbling and the cheese golden.

This richly flavoured ragout can be cooked on top of the stove or in the oven. It's a longish shopping list but a simple method, and the various meats all add a lovely complexity of flavour. Whilst it's great with pasta it's also good with creamy mashed potatoes or soft polenta.

PORK, CHICKEN AND CHICKEN LIVER RAGOUT **FOR 6 MAIN COURSES**

2 onions, peeled and thinly sliced
50 g unsalted butter
4 cloves garlic, peeled and chopped
½ red chilli, finely chopped
2 bay leaves
12 sage leaves, chopped
1 tbsp fresh thyme leaves
2 tbsp extra virgin olive oil
300 g boneless and skinless chicken
   thighs, thickly sliced
300 g lean pork mince
60 g tomato paste
400 g chopped tomatoes, fresh or
   canned
300 ml red wine
4 tbsp soy sauce
150 g chicken livers or duck livers,
   cleaned and roughly chopped
500 g dried pasta (penne, fusilli or
   macaroni work well)
salt and freshly ground black pepper
100 g Parmesan, grated

1. Sauté the onions in the butter over low heat until softened and completely collapsed. Add the garlic, chilli and herbs and cook for another 5 minutes with the lid on.

2. Tip the mixture into a bowl, then put the pan back on the heat; there's no need to clean it out.

3. Add 1 tbsp olive oil and sauté the chicken until coloured, then place in the bowl with the onions.

4. Add remaining olive oil and pork mince to the pan and cook until browned.

5. Return the chicken and onion mixture to the pan along with the tomato paste, chopped tomatoes, wine and soy sauce and bring to a boil.

6. Put the lid on and simmer over a gentle heat for 1 hour, stirring occasionally, or bake in the oven at 150°C.

7. Stir in the livers and cook for another 15 minutes.

8. Cook the pasta until al dente, then drain.

9. Taste the ragout for seasoning, then mix in half the cheese.

10. Divide the pasta among six plates, spoon the ragout on top and sprinkle with the remaining cheese.

Using a mixture of different-coloured tomatoes looks really pretty. Any type of pasta will work with this, whether something long like spaghetti or more tubular like macaroni.

CHERRY TOMATO, PANCETTA AND THYME PASTA **FOR 4 MAIN COURSES**

1 red onion, peeled and thinly sliced

4 cloves garlic, peeled and sliced

¼ red chilli, sliced (more or less to taste)

200 g pancetta, lardons or belly bacon, diced

3 tbsp olive oil

300 g cherry tomatoes

2 tsp fresh thyme

2 spring onions, cut on an angle into 3 cm lengths

400 g dried pasta

freshly ground black pepper

sea salt

60 g Parmesan, grated

1. Sauté the onion, garlic, chilli and pancetta in the olive oil until the onion begins to caramelize, stirring often to prevent sticking.

2. Add the cherry tomatoes, thyme and spring onions and cook until the tomatoes are just beginning to pop, stirring as it cooks. Take off the heat and keep warm.

3. Cook the pasta in lightly salted water until al dente. Drain in a colander, then toss with the tomato mixture, seasoning with pepper and sea salt.

4. Divide among four warm bowls and sprinkle with the Parmesan.

This simple dish is quite rich, so works better as a starter than as a main course. Choose a strong-flavoured, firm-ish blue cheese that won't break up too much, and any type of short pasta.

PASTA WITH BLUE CHEESE, WALNUTS AND PEAR **FOR 4 STARTERS**

250 g dried pasta
1 onion, peeled and thinly sliced
2 tbsp olive oil
2 firm, ripe pears
80 g walnut pieces, lightly toasted
120 g blue cheese
salt and freshly ground black pepper

1. Cook the pasta in lightly salted water until al dente.

2. While it's cooking, sauté the onion in the oil, stirring often, until beginning to caramelize.

3. Peel the pears, cut into quarters and remove the core, then thinly slice them. Add to the onion, gently stirring, and cook over low heat for 2 minutes.

4. Add the nuts and blue cheese, turn heat off and put a lid on to keep it all warm.

5. Drain the pasta in a colander, then tip into a warmed large bowl. Tip on the pear mixture and toss it gently together. Taste for seasoning.

6. Serve in warmed bowls.

CHAPTER FOUR

LIGHT MEALS AND SALADS

These toasts are reminiscent of Chinese restaurants around the Western world. It's important to use medium to large raw prawn tail meat or they simply will not work. I spread half the mixture on sandwich bread and the rest on sliced baguette – it's up to you which you prefer. These are great served with sweet chilli sauce.

PRAWN AND SESAME TOASTS
MAKES 16 TOASTS, SERVE 2-3 PER PERSON AS A SNACK

250 g raw prawn tails, shells removed, cut into chunks
2 spring onions, sliced
2 tsp cornflour
2 tsp fish sauce or soy sauce, or ½ tsp salt
3 tbsp sesame seeds, toasted
8 slices white sandwich bread, crusts removed (or 16 slices baguette, ½ cm thick)
vegetable oil, for deep-frying

1. Preheat the oven to 100°C.

2. Place the prawn tails, spring onions, cornflour, fish sauce or soy sauce or salt and half the sesame seeds in a food processor.

3. Blitz until smooth, then spread the mixture evenly over the sandwich bread and cut each slice in half on a diagonal to give triangles, or simply spread on the sliced baguette.

4. Scatter the remaining sesame seeds onto the prawn mixture.

5. Heat 4 cm of oil to 180°C in a wide pan (or use a deep-fryer) and fry the toasts in several batches until they're golden on both sides. Remove from the oil, drain on kitchen paper and keep warm on a baking tray in the oven while you cook the rest.

6. Serve piping hot.

The chicken is cooked in a Chinese fashion: poached and left to rest in the hot 'stock'
which finishes cooking it gently and keeps it juicy. The stock from it will be delicious –
you can freeze it for later use or use within a few days in soups, risottos or stews.

POACHED CHICKEN SALAD WITH GREEN BEANS, PEACHES AND PECANS **FOR 6 MAIN COURSES**

1 large chicken (about 1.5 kg); buy the best-quality bird you can afford

300 ml white wine (not too sweet)

2 bay leaves

2 thumbs ginger, skin scrubbed and finely sliced

1 handful of your favourite herbs

2 onions, peeled and quartered

flaky sea salt

peel and juice of 2 tangerines

peel of 1 lemon and juice of 2 lemons

6 peaches

250 g fine green beans, blanched and refreshed

150 g pecan nuts, toasted

50 ml olive oil

1 tbsp honey

2 tsp grain mustard

1. Place the chicken in a deep pot with the next five ingredients, a few teaspoons of flaky salt and the peel from the tangerines and lemon.

2. Cover with cold water and bring to a gentle boil, skimming off any foam that rises.

3. Put a lid on and cook at a rapid simmer for 30 minutes. Take off the heat and leave to cool with the lid on. It's important you keep the lid on to ensure the chicken cooks through.

4. Take the chicken from the stock and peel the skin off the bird, discarding it. Pull the legs from the carcass and remove any meat, tearing it into thick strips; likewise remove the breast meat from the carcass and tear that into thick strips. Put the meat in a bowl.

5. Spoon a few tablespoons of the stock over the chicken.

6. Remove the stones from the peaches, cut into wedges and add to the chicken along with the beans and pecans.

7. Mix the olive oil with the reserved citrus juices, honey, mustard and salt to taste.

8. To serve, pour the dressing over the chicken, toss and divide among six bowls or plates.

This simple meatloaf is truly delicious. It's flavoured with baked beans – what could be tastier? I used a mixture of venison and beef, but you can make it with any lean meat. Garam masala spice mix works really well in this, but you could just use mixed spice, five-spice, allspice or 1 teaspoon of ground cinnamon.

BEEF AND BAKED BEAN MEATLOAF

FOR 6-8 MAIN COURSES

10 rashers smoked streaky bacon
500 g minced venison
500 g minced beef
2 onions, peeled and diced or grated
4 cloves garlic, peeled and chopped
4 tbsp grain mustard
50 g breadcrumbs
300–400 g tinned baked beans
2 tsp garam masala
2 tsp dried oregano or dried mixed
   herbs
400 g chopped peeled tomatoes, fresh or
   canned
salt and freshly ground black pepper

1. Preheat oven to 170°C. Line a deep-sided 2-litre terrine or loaf tin with baking paper, making sure there's plenty overlapping. Alternatively, cut open an oven bag and use this to line the tin.

2. Line the base and sides with the bacon, also letting it hang over the sides.

3. Mix everything together except the tomatoes and season with 2 scant tsp salt and plenty of pepper. Place the mixture in the tin and press it flat.

4. Pour on the tomato, then fold the bacon overhang over them.

5. Fold over the overhanging baking paper or oven bag, then seal tightly with foil.

6. Sit in a roasting dish (the juices will bubble out a little) and bake in the centre of the oven for 1 hour.

7. Peel off the foil and turn the temperature up to 200°C. Continue cooking for another 15 minutes.

8. Take from the oven and leave to rest in the tin for at least 20 minutes before turning out.

9. To serve, either eat this hot from the oven served with vegetables, or leave it to go cold and serve sliced, as you would a terrine, with salad and chutney as a starter.

The first time I heard about this Tuscan salad I wasn't convinced. Stale bread, soaked in water and tossed with tomatoes just didn't sound like a good idea. However, it's wonderfully flavoursome and a good way to use up leftover bread and a-little-too-soft tomatoes. It's great on its own or served with grilled tuna, prawns, cold poached chicken ... in fact anything. Sourdough, ciabatta and firm country-style bread work best.

PANZANELLA **FOR 4–6 AS A SIDE DISH OR STARTER**

500 g slightly stale bread, cut into large
   cubes
100 ml extra virgin olive oil
50 ml red wine vinegar
1 large red onion, peeled and thinly
   sliced
4 very ripe tomatoes, roughly chopped
1 small cucumber, roughly chopped
1 handful parsley, chopped
1 handful basil leaves, torn
1 handful mint leaves
2 tbsp baby capers
1 handful pitted olives, chopped
salt and freshly ground black pepper

1. Soak the bread in cold water for 10 minutes, then squeeze the water out and place the bread in a large bowl.

2. Pour on the oil and vinegar and toss well.

3. Add the onion, tomatoes and cucumber and mix in.

4. Leave for 30 minutes, then add the herbs, capers and olives and mix again.

5. Leave for 10 minutes before mixing one last time, tasting for seasoning and serving.

For this recipe, I used canned butter beans as it was much quicker to make, but by all means soak and cook your own beans. Serve with couscous, rice, mashed potatoes or pasta.

LAMB MEATBALLS WITH TOMATO, BUTTER BEANS AND BACON **FOR 6 MAIN COURSES**

800 g finely minced lean lamb

1 tsp dried rubbed mint or 1 tbsp shredded fresh mint

1 carrot, peeled and grated

4 tbsp cold water

salt and freshly ground black pepper

100 g flour

vegetable oil, for cooking

8 cloves garlic, peeled and thickly sliced

1 tbsp fresh rosemary leaves

1 large onion, peeled and thinly sliced

200 g bacon lardons or thickly sliced streaky bacon, diced

750 ml tomato passata or diced or chopped peeled tomatoes

1 x 400 g tin butter beans, drained and rinsed

200 ml water

chopped parsley, to garnish

1. In a large bowl, mix the lamb, mint and carrot together with the cold water, 1 scant tsp salt and plenty of coarsely ground pepper.

2. Divide the mixture into four even-sized portions, then each portion into six. Roll into balls and toss in the flour to coat.

3. Heat a wide, deep pot with a few tablespoons of vegetable oil. When hot, add as many meatballs as will fit in without crowding. Brown all over, then remove with a slotted spoon onto a platter while you cook the rest, adding a little extra oil if needed.

4. Once the last batch is cooked and removed, add the sliced garlic, rosemary and onion to the pan and cook until caramelized, stirring frequently and scraping the cooked bits off the bottom of the pan.

5. Add the bacon and cook over moderate heat, stirring frequently, until golden.

6. Add the passata, butter beans and the 200 ml water. Bring to the boil, stirring as it heats up.

7. Return the meatballs to the bubbling sauce, stirring gently as you do. If the meatballs aren't covered with sauce, top it up with hot water.

8. Turn to a rapid simmer and cook for 25 minutes with a lid on.

9. Taste for seasoning, then serve scattered with parsley.

I was given this recipe by a Tunisian colleague many years ago and, much like the better-known Italian Panzanella salad (see page 105), this recipe was likely created to use up leftover bread. I used Turkish pide bread, but you could use Indian naan or Italian ciabatta – it doesn't matter if it's very thin or more fluffy, it just needs to be baked crisp.

TUNISIAN BREAD SALAD FOR 4-6 AS A SIDE DISH

250 g slightly stale bread
flaky sea salt
150 ml extra virgin olive oil
2 red onions, peeled and thinly sliced
    into rings
50 ml red wine vinegar or lemon juice
400 g cherry tomatoes, halved
4 spring onions, sliced
salt and freshly ground black pepper
1 handful flat parsley leaves
1 small handful basil leaves

1. Preheat oven to 180°C.

2. Tear the bread into pieces and place in a roasting dish. Sprinkle liberally with flaky sea salt, drizzle with half the oil and toss well. Bake for 10 minutes. Toss again, then cook until the bread is crisp and golden. Remove from the oven and cool.

3. Mix the onions with the vinegar or lemon juice in a large bowl. After 10 minutes, add the tomatoes and spring onions and season.

4. Add the toasted bread and herbs and toss together, then leave for 5 minutes.

5. To serve, toss again and it's ready.

This is a good winter lunch dish or it can be made as a first course and served more like a 'soup with dumplings'. If this is how you'd prefer to serve it, add an extra 400 ml of stock and you'll have enough to serve eight bowls of soup.

CHORIZO DUMPLINGS IN CHICKPEA STEW

FOR 4 LUNCHES

300 g cooking chorizo, peeled and sliced

400 g coarse lean pork mince

3 spring onions, sliced

2 tsp cumin seeds, lightly toasted

1 tsp fine salt

3 tbsp flour

oil, for frying

2 onions, peeled and sliced

8 cloves garlic, peeled and sliced

1 tbsp chopped fresh rosemary

300 g cooked chickpeas, drained and rinsed (from a can is fine)

300 g cooked butter beans, drained and rinsed (from a can is fine)

600 ml chicken or vegetable stock

1 handful parsley, chopped

1 tbsp sherry vinegar, cider vinegar or red wine vinegar

salt and freshly ground black pepper

1. Put the chorizo in a food processor and pulse for 5 seconds. Add the mince and pulse for another 10 seconds.

2. Add the spring onions, cumin seeds and salt and blitz again to incorporate.

3. Tip the mixture onto a lightly floured board and halve it, then divide each half into eight even-sized pieces. Roll into balls and toss in the flour to coat.

4. Heat up a pan with 3 mm cooking oil, then fry the dumplings in several batches until golden all over. Set aside.

5. Don't clean the pan, but add the onions, garlic and rosemary and cook until the onions are caramelized.

6. Add the chickpeas, butter beans and stock and bring to the boil, stirring as it comes up to heat, then turn to a simmer. Place a lid on the pan and gently boil for 10 minutes.

7. Add the dumplings to the stew and bring back to the boil before reducing to a simmer. Place the lid back on and cook for a further 15 minutes.

8. Take off the heat, stir in the parsley and vinegar, taste for seasoning and serve straight away.

This salad is a great way to show off Israeli couscous – also known as Sardinian fregola or mograbiah in Arab stores. It's really important you toast it quite dark to give it a lovely nutty flavour. This is a wonderful salad in its own right, but also terrific as an accompaniment to grilled or roast meats or fish.

ISRAELI COUSCOUS, BROAD BEAN AND PISTACHIO SALAD **FOR 6 STARTERS**

4 tbsp extra virgin olive oil

200 g Israeli couscous

1 large red onion, peeled and thinly sliced

2 cloves garlic, peeled and sliced

500 ml hot water

1 tsp flaky salt

200 g broad beans, podded and skins removed if large (frozen are fine)

1 large handful picked flat parsley leaves

1 large handful mint leaves (tear the large ones)

2 tbsp chopped dill

4 spring onions, sliced

salt and freshly ground black pepper

100 g pistachio nuts, lightly toasted and roughly chopped

1 juicy lemon, cut in half

1. Heat up a saucepan and add half the oil. Add the couscous and fry over a moderate high heat for 4–5 minutes, stirring frequently to prevent the grains burning, until dark golden. Once done, tip into a heatproof bowl.

2. Place the remaining oil in the saucepan and add the onion and garlic. Cook over a moderate heat until caramelized.

3. Return the couscous to the pan, pour on hot water and flaky salt and bring to the boil. Boil for exactly 6 minutes, then put a lid on and take off the heat. Leave to cool.

4. Mix in the broad beans, parsley, mint, dill and spring onions and taste for seasoning.

5. Sprinkle with the nuts and squeeze the lemon juice over just before you serve it.

A Spanish tortilla is more similar to the Italian frittata than the Mexican tortilla,
which is more of a 'wrap'. I came up with this combination as a way to use up leftover
Christmas ham one year, but it has since been a good way to use up any leftover meat
from a dinner party.

HAM, GARLIC AND POTATO TORTILLA
FOR 4 MAIN COURSES

350 g potatoes, cut into 2 cm dice (no
   need to peel them, just scrub the
   skins)
120 ml olive oil
500 g cooked ham, sliced (or turkey or
   chicken meat)
6 cloves garlic, peeled and sliced
8 eggs
1 small bunch parsley, shredded, plus
   extra to garnish
2 spring onions, sliced
salt and freshly ground black pepper

1. Boil or steam the potatoes until cooked, then drain in a colander.

2. Heat up a heavy-based 25–30 cm pan (ideally non-stick) and add one-third of the oil. When it's hot, add the potatoes and cook until golden, tossing occasionally.

3. Tip into a bowl and add another third of the oil to the pan.

4. Add the ham and garlic to the pan and fry to colour, then put in the bowl with the potatoes.

5. Add the eggs, parsley and spring onions to the potatoes. Season with salt and pepper and mix well.

6. Put the pan back on the heat, and when it's hot add the remaining oil and count to 10.

7. Pour in the egg mixture and count to 20. Using a spatula, scrape the outer edges into the centre and move the uncooked centre to the outside. Do this for about 20 seconds, then either place the pan under a grill, bake in an oven at 180°C or place a lid on the pan and turn the heat down, and cook until the egg has set completely.

8. Leave to sit in the pan for 5 minutes, then invert onto a plate.

9. To serve, garnish with parsley and cut into wedges or small squares if eating as a snack.

This salad also works well made with sweet potato instead of new potatoes, and cold-smoked salmon instead of hot-smoked, or even smoked chicken or duck breast.

HOT-SMOKED SALMON, POTATO AND PEA SALAD WITH TAHINI YOGHURT DRESSING FOR 4 MAIN COURSES

2 small red onions, peeled and sliced
   into thin rings
3 tbsp white vinegar or lemon juice
600 g new potatoes
3 tbsp extra virgin olive oil
1 tsp cumin
salt and freshly ground black pepper
4 tsp tahini
3 tbsp plain yoghurt
2 tbsp cold water
2 large handfuls salad leaves
150 g peas, blanched and refreshed
1 cup mixed olives
600 g hot-smoked salmon fillet, skin
   and bones removed
1 tbsp sesame seeds, toasted

1. Rinse the onion rings in cold water for a few minutes, then drain and place in a bowl. Pour on the vinegar or lemon juice and mix, then leave for 30 minutes, tossing once more.

2. Meanwhile, boil the potatoes in lightly salted water until cooked. Drain, and when cool enough to handle cut in half lengthways and put in a bowl.

3. Heat a small pan with 1 tbsp oil and the cumin. Cook until aromatic, then pour over the potatoes with some pepper and salt and mix it all together.

4. Mix the tahini and yoghurt together in a small bowl, then pour in half the vinegar from the onions, the water and the remaining olive oil. Taste for seasoning.

5. To serve, toss the onions and vinegar marinade with the potatoes and divide among four plates. Scatter with the leaves, peas and olives and flake the salmon on top. Finally, spoon over the dressing and sesame seeds.

I prefer to use the gorgeous golden Zespri kiwifruit in the salad, but the more familiar green ones are also delicious. Roast a chicken yourself or, if you're in a hurry, buy one already cooked.

CHICKEN, KIWIFRUIT AND SWEET POTATO SALAD **FOR 6 MAIN COURSES**

500 g sweet potato, peeled and diced
4 tbsp extra virgin olive oil
salt and freshly ground black pepper
hot water
1 good handful fresh herbs off the
    stem (basil, dill, tarragon, parsley,
    coriander)
1 red onion, peeled and thinly sliced
1 head fennel, thinly sliced (discard the
    thick base)
4 tbsp lemon juice
4 tsp runny honey (New Zealand
    manuka honey works well)
2 tbsp light soy sauce or ¼ tsp salt
4 kiwifruit
1 roast chicken
1 large bunch watercress or rocket,
    washed and drained

1. Preheat oven to 200°C.

2. Put the sweet potato and half the olive oil in a roasting dish, season and toss, then drizzle on a few tablespoons of hot water. Roast until golden, tossing several times.

3. Leave to cool, then toss with the herbs.

4. Mix the onion and fennel with half the lemon juice and leave to 'cure' for 20 minutes.

5. Mix the remaining lemon juice with the honey until it dissolves, then mix in the remaining olive oil and the soy or salt.

6. Peel the kiwifruit and cut into chunks.

7. Remove all the meat from the chicken and break or slice into chunks.

8. To serve, toss the sweet potato with the watercress or rocket and kiwifruit and divide among your plates. Lay the chunks of chicken over the top, then pile on the fennel onion salad. Stir the dressing again and drizzle it over.

This is a wonderful first course to serve at a dinner party. Or you can make them into flash canapés by serving in shot glasses with the avocado in the bottom and the tomato jelly and thinly sliced prawn tails on top. You'll need to make them at least 8 hours in advance to allow them to set properly, but they must be eaten within 24 hours or the avocado can discolour.

AVOCADO MOUSSE WITH TOMATO JELLY AND PRAWNS   FOR 4-6 STARTERS

3 very ripe tomatoes (you may need more; enough for 220 ml purée)

½ clove garlic, peeled

salt and freshly ground black pepper

2 tsp sherry vinegar or red wine vinegar

4½ leaves gelatine

280 g avocado flesh (about 1½ avocados)

2 tbsp avocado oil or extra virgin olive oil

200 g low-fat Greek-style yoghurt

2 drops Tabasco sauce

1½ tbsp lemon juice

50 ml water

200 g cooked prawn tails, out of the shell

1 lemon, cut into wedges

1. Cut the tomatoes into quarters and place in a blender with the garlic, ¼ tsp salt and a few grinds of pepper. Purée well, then pass through a fine sieve.

2. Take 220 ml of the purée and mix in the vinegar. Pour 80 ml into a small pan and gently warm it through. Soak 2 leaves gelatine in very cold water for 4 minutes. Remove and gently squeeze out excess water, then add to the warm tomato purée and stir until dissolved. Mix into the rest of the purée, then divide among 4 x 200 ml or 6 x 150 ml jelly moulds. Place on a tray in the fridge until set, about 1½ hours.

3. Once they're ready, make the mousse. Put the avocado flesh, oil, yoghurt and Tabasco in a food processor and purée until smooth, then tip into a bowl.

4. Put the lemon juice in a small pan with the water and bring to a simmer, then keep warm. Soak the remaining 2½ leaves of gelatine in very cold water for 4 minutes. Remove and gently squeeze out excess water, then add to the warm lemon juice and stir until dissolved. Whisk this into the avocado purée and taste for seasoning. Spoon the mousse on top of the tomato jelly, then cover and place in the fridge until set – around 6 hours.

5. To serve, dip the moulds briefly into hot water and invert on a plate. Hold the mould firmly and shake jelly out gently onto the plate. Sit the prawn tails next to the jelly and serve with a lemon wedge.

This is an incredibly simple, tasty and refreshing salad. The lime and watermelon go very well together and the prawns and watermelon even better – who knew?!

PRAWN, WATERMELON AND LIME SALAD **FOR 4 STARTERS**

400 g (12–16) uncooked peeled prawn
   tails (with the tail intact)
1 tbsp olive oil
salt and freshly ground black pepper
2 limes
1 tbsp mirin or 1 tsp caster sugar
¼ watermelon (about 600 g), rind cut
   off
50 g roasted unsalted peanuts, crushed
1 handful coriander leaves

1. Lay the prawns between kitchen paper and pat them dry, then brush with 1 tsp oil and a little salt and pepper. Heat a pan and cook the prawns on both sides for about a minute each side — cooking time will depend on their size. Leave on a plate to cool.

2. Cut the skin and pith from one of the limes and remove the segments, then dice the flesh. Mix with the mirin or sugar and the remaining olive oil and leave for 5 minutes.

3. Cut the remaining lime into wedges, then cut the watermelon into chunks.

4. To serve, place the watermelon on four plates and sit the prawns on top. Spoon on the diced lime dressing, the peanuts and the coriander, then tuck in a lime wedge.

This is a classic salad created in the 1890s at the Waldorf Hotel (as it was then called) in New York. The reason it's a classic is that the combination of ingredients work wonderfully – even after so many years.

CHICKEN WALDORF SALAD FOR 4 MAIN COURSES

4 chicken breasts, with skin on (you can remove it once it's cooked but it helps keep the meat moist)
1 tsp olive oil
salt and freshly ground black pepper
4 tbsp mayonnaise
2 tbsp crème fraîche or sour cream
2 x 20-cm stalks celery, washed and sliced
2 baby cos or baby gem lettuces, leaves separated
2 endives, base cut off and leaves separated (either red or white endive is ok)
60 g walnut halves, toasted
2 apples (use something slightly sour like a Granny Smith)

1. Preheat oven to 170°C.

2. Brush the chicken breasts with the oil and lightly season.

3. Heat an ovenproof pan over moderate heat and place the breasts in, skin-side facing down. Cook until the skin becomes golden, then turn over and cook for 2 minutes on the other side.

4. Place in the oven and roast until they're cooked through; around 12–15 minutes. Remove from the oven and leave to cool.

5. Mix the mayonnaise and crème fraîche or sour cream in a large bowl.

6. Add the celery, lettuce, endive and half the walnuts.

7. Cut the apples into quarters and remove the core. Slice ½ cm thick, then cut the slices into matchsticks and add to the bowl.

8. Remove the skin from the chicken, if you prefer, and slice the breasts.

9. Add to the bowl and toss everything together, seasoning to taste.

10. To serve, divide the salad among four bowls and scatter with the remaining walnuts.

Lots of fresh flavours and crunchy textures in this salad make it the perfect summer supper. You may think this is a lot of tarragon in a salad but, believe me, it works very well.

POACHED CHICKEN, TARRAGON, PEAR AND GRAPE SALAD **FOR 4 MAIN COURSES**

olive oil

4 chicken breasts

1 small handful herbs (rosemary, thyme, oregano, or a mixture)

salt and freshly ground black pepper

½ wine glass white wine

hot water

1 juicy orange

2 tbsp pomegranate molasses (or a mixture of honey and balsamic vinegar)

2 ripe pears

½ bunch grapes, halved

1 large handful green beans, blanched and refreshed

1 medium iceberg lettuce, core removed, shredded ½ cm thick

2 tbsp tarragon leaves

1. Put a saucepan large enough to hold the breasts in one layer over medium-high heat. Add the oil and cook the chicken breasts until golden on both sides. Add the herbs and season well. Pour on the wine and let it boil for 1 minute. Pour on enough hot water to barely cover the chicken and bring almost to the boil, then turn to a simmer. Put a lid on the pan and cook for 10 minutes.

2. Turn the heat off and leave to cool in the liquid for 30 minutes.

3. Juice the orange and mix with the pomegranate molasses and 3 tbsp olive oil in a large salad bowl.

4. Quarter the pears and remove the core. Slice ½ cm thick and add to the dressing along with the grapes, beans, lettuce and tarragon.

5. Take the chicken from the poaching liquid and slice into ½ cm thick strips. Add to the salad.

6. Toss everything together and serve.

*This is a lovely starter, full of the richness of caramelized onions, flavoursome duck livers
(although chicken livers work just as well and may be easier to source) and the tang of
oranges. Pecan nuts add texture, too.*

DUCK LIVER SALAD WITH PECANS, ORANGE AND RADISH **FOR 4 STARTERS**

300 g duck livers
salt and freshly ground black pepper
30 g butter
1 small onion, peeled and thinly sliced
2 strips orange peel, julienned
2 tbsp balsamic vinegar
2 tsp soy sauce
2 tbsp orange juice (squeeze the
    membranes after you've removed the
    segments)
2 handfuls salad leaves
2 oranges, peeled and segmented
    avoiding membranes and pith
16 pecans, toasted and roughly chopped
6 radishes, thinly sliced

1. Remove any sinews, fat or entrails from the livers, keeping them whole rather than
cutting them up too small, then lightly season.

2. Place a wide pan on to heat and add the butter and cook until sizzling. Add the
sliced onion and orange peel and sauté until caramelized, stirring often.

3. Add the livers and cook for 10 seconds on each side.

4. Add the vinegar, soy sauce and orange juice and bring to a simmer. Cook for
1 minute (less if the livers are small).

5. To serve, divide the salad leaves among four plates and scatter on half the orange
segments and pecans. Spoon the livers and their cooking juices on top, then scatter
the remaining orange segments and pecans on along with the radishes.

These very basic fish cakes are made from hot-smoked salmon – although any hot-smoked fish, such as mackerel or cod, will do. Serve them just as they are or with steamed greens and salad for a lunch or supper meal. This recipe makes eight large fishcakes – allow two per main course.

HOT-SMOKED SALMON CAKES WITH DILL MUSTARD DRESSING **FOR 4 MAIN COURSES**

500 g boiling potatoes, peeled and
 quartered
1 red onion, peeled and thinly sliced
salt and freshly ground black pepper
3 tbsp grain mustard
2 tbsp brown sugar
1 tbsp white vinegar
3 tbsp roughly chopped dill
4 tbsp self-raising flour (plus extra for
 dusting the fish cakes)
250 g hot-smoked salmon, skin and
 bones removed
1 handful roughly chopped parsley
vegetable oil, for cooking (or butter and
 oil together)
rocket or watercress
1 lemon, cut into quarters, to garnish

1. Put the potatoes and half the sliced onion in a pot and cover with cold water. Season with salt and pepper and gently boil until the potatoes are cooked.

2. While the potatoes are cooking, mix the mustard, sugar, vinegar and dill together and put to one side.

3. Drain the potatoes well, making sure as much moisture as possible is drained off. Return to the pot and mash, then mix in the flour.

4. Flake the salmon and add this, along with the remaining sliced onion and the parsley, and mix it all together. Taste for seasoning and adjust if necessary.

5. Once cool enough to handle, divide into eight and roll into balls. Flatten into barrel shapes then dust generously with more flour.

6. Heat up a pan and add 5 mm oil or a mixture of butter and oil.

7. Add as many fishcakes as will fit comfortably into the pan and cook until golden.

8. Gently flip them over and cook on the other side until heated through. It may be easier to colour them in the pan then cook on a baking paper-lined tray in an oven set at 120°C until warmed through (5–8 minutes, depending on their size).

9. To serve, sit the fishcakes on warmed plates and garnish with the rocket or watercress and lemon, then drizzle with the dill mustard dressing and serve with lemon wedges.

The combination of slightly salty cheese and sweet cherry tomatoes is terrific – especially with the basil added. If your haloumi is very firm and salty, place in a heatproof bowl, pour very hot water over it and leave to cool in the water before preparing. This method softens it and makes it much more palatable.

VINE LEAF-WRAPPED HALOUMI WITH TOMATO CHILLI SALSA FOR 4 STARTERS

300 g haloumi, sliced into 8
16–24 vine leaves in brine (try a Greek or Turkish shop)
150 g cherry tomatoes, quartered
¼ red chilli, thinly sliced into rings
1 small handful basil leaves, shredded
1 tbsp extra virgin olive oil
2 tsp lemon juice
salt and freshly ground black pepper
vegetable oil, for frying

1. Pat the cheese dry. Depending on the size of the vine leaves, lay 2–3 of them on a bench, slightly overlapping. Sit a piece of haloumi in the centre of the leaves, then fold the leaves nearest you over the cheese and roll it up, tucking in the edges as though it were a parcel. Do the same to the rest of the haloumi and place on a cloth to absorb excess moisture.

2. In a bowl, mix together all the remaining ingredients (except the vegetable oil). Season lightly as the cheese can be a little salty. Set aside.

3. Heat a frying pan with a few tablespoons of vegetable oil, then carefully sit in enough haloumi bundles to fit comfortably – don't overcrowd them. Fry over medium-high heat until the leaves colour, then carefully flip them over. Cook all the bundles in this way. You might like to keep them warm in an oven set at 100°C.

4. Serve while still warm with the salsa spooned on top.

*These little tarts make a tasty snack to serve with drinks, or you could make one large
one for lunch and serve it with salad. Sun-blushed tomatoes are sometimes called semi-
dried, and the nicest ones come marinated in olive oil. If you don't like goat's cheese, then
use feta, Cheddar or even a blue cheese.*

LEEK, OLIVE AND GOAT'S CHEESE TARTS WITH SUN-BLUSHED TOMATO DRESSING MAKES 12 TARTS

a little butter
400 g short crust pastry (see page 176)
4 tbsp extra virgin olive oil
1 leek, approximately 200 g, rinsed and
   thinly sliced
1 egg
1 tbsp tarragon leaves
12 pitted green olives, roughly chopped
80 g goat's cheese, grated or crumbled
   (both soft and hard will work)
80 g sun-blushed tomatoes
2 tbsp lemon juice

1. Preheat oven to 180°C. Lightly butter 12 smallish muffin tins or a muffin tray.

2. Roll the pastry out 3 mm thick. Use a pastry cutter to cut out 12 circles of pastry larger than the tins you're using. Press these into the muffin tins, making sure the pastry comes up to just above the lip of each cavity. Put in the fridge to firm up for at least 30 minutes.

3. Heat half the oil in a pan and sauté the leek over a really low heat until it has softened completely, keeping a lid on the pan and stirring often. Once it's ready, take the lid off the pan and continue to cook to dry the mixture out a little.

4. Take from the heat and leave to cool for a few minutes, then mix in the egg, tarragon, olives and cheese.

5. Spoon this into the pastry cases and bake until golden, around 20 minutes.

6. While they're cooking, place the tomatoes in a small food processor or blender or use a stick blender. Add the lemon juice and remaining oil and blitz to give a slightly lumpy purée.

7. To serve, remove the warm tarts from the tray and drizzle with the dressing.

This delicious, healthy-tasting salad is great as a side dish to serve with fish or poultry, and also on its own as a salad starter. Use a variety of mushrooms for interesting appearance and texture.

RAW MUSHROOM AND RED CABBAGE SALAD WITH YOGHURT DRESSING **FOR 4 STARTERS**

100 g button mushrooms, thinly sliced

100 g shiitake mushrooms, stalks discarded, caps thinly sliced

100 g oyster mushrooms, thinly sliced

2 tbsp lime juice

2 tsp soy sauce

1 clove garlic, peeled and finely chopped or crushed

2 tbsp lemon juice

3 tbsp extra virgin olive oil

¼ red cabbage (about 150 g), core removed, very thinly shredded

2 tbsp cider vinegar

1 tsp caster sugar

100 ml plain yoghurt

50 ml vegetable oil

salt and freshly ground black pepper

1 handful basil leaves

1. Place the button and shiitake mushrooms in one bowl, and the oyster mushrooms in another.

2. Add the lime juice and soy sauce to the button and shiitake mushrooms.

3. Add the garlic and 1 tbsp lemon juice to the oyster mushrooms.

4. Add half the olive oil to each bowl, then mix and leave to marinate for at least 2 hours, preferably 6–8, covered in the fridge.

5. Mix the cabbage with the vinegar and sugar and leave to marinate for the same amount of time as the mushrooms, covered, in the fridge. Give the mushrooms and cabbage a toss several times.

6. Whisk the remaining lemon juice with the yoghurt and vegetable oil and season with salt and pepper.

7. To serve, toss the mushrooms together and drain the juice from them. Tear the basil leaves and mix with the cabbage. Divide the cabbage among your plates, then sit the mushrooms on top. Give the yoghurt dressing another stir, then drizzle over the salad.

As a starter this dish is light and refreshing and also very delicious. By baking the ricotta in this way it becomes firmer and much more tasty.

PARMESAN BAKED RICOTTA WITH CHILLI ROAST TOMATOES AND PEAS FOR 4 STARTERS

200 g ricotta
salt and freshly ground black pepper
2 tbsp Parmesan, finely grated
½ tsp fresh thyme leaves
2 generous pinches cumin seeds
extra virgin olive oil
16 cherry tomatoes
¼ tsp dried chilli flakes (or finely
   chopped fresh red chilli)
80 g cooked peas
1 handful basil leaves
1 large handful mixed salad leaves

1. Preheat oven to 190°C.

2. Cut the ricotta into four pieces of equal thickness, lay on a baking tray lined with baking paper and sprinkle with a little salt. If you're using ricotta from a round tub, cut it horizontally into four.

3. Mix together the Parmesan, thyme, cumin seeds and 2 tbsp oil, then spoon it over the ricotta, spreading it evenly.

4. Bake in the upper part of the oven for 18–20 minutes until golden, then take out and cool.

5. While the ricotta is cooking, slice the tomatoes in half horizontally and sprinkle with the chilli, some salt and olive oil. Bake in the oven until beginning to colour, around 25 minutes.

6. Take from the oven and leave to cool.

7. Smash a quarter of the peas lightly using a mortar and pestle, or place them in a plastic bag and hit with a rolling pin. Tear the basil leaves into pieces and add to the whole and smashed peas with 2 tbsp oil, salt and pepper.

8. To serve, place a slice of ricotta on a plate and scatter with the salad leaves. Sit 8 tomato halves on and drizzle with the pea salad and any of the oil from the cheese or tomato baking trays.

Honestly, these tarts couldn't be easier. You can also add diced cheese, chopped fresh herbs or garlic, if you want to fancy them up a bit. Lovely taken on a picnic or served with salad.

SPINACH AND BACON TARTS

MAKES 4 x 10 cm TARTS

4–6 sheets filo pastry
30 g butter, melted (you may need more), plus extra for greasing tins
200 g smoked streaky bacon, cut into 2 cm pieces
350 g spinach
1 egg, plus 1 egg yolk
freshly ground black pepper and a little salt

1. Preheat oven to 180°C. Butter four 10 cm fluted tart tins (or similar) generously, then put in the fridge to set the butter.

2. Cut the filo into 15 cm squares – this doesn't have to be exact and a little overhang looks fine. You want three squares per tart. Lay one piece down and butter it, lay another square on top, butter that, then add a last square and butter. Press the layered pastry into the tart tin, making sure the bottom has no air bubbles in it.

3. Cook the bacon until quite crispy either by grilling or frying it. Drain off excess fat.

4. Bring a pot of lightly salted water to the boil, add the spinach and stir it around for a few seconds. After 30 seconds drain in a colander and gently run cold water over it. Once it's cool enough to handle, squeeze out excess water. You want around 200 g cooked spinach.

5. Put the bacon in a food processor and blitz to coarse crumbs, then put in a bowl. Don't clean out the processor.

6. Put the spinach and eggs into the processor and blitz to a coarse purée. Add to the bacon and mix it all together. Add very little salt, as the bacon should be salty enough, but plenty of pepper.

7. Divide the filling among the tarts and fold the pastry back over the filling, keeping some of it exposed. Brush the tarts with the remaining butter, then bake until the pastry is golden and crisp; around 20 minutes.

This chunky, healthy salad is great as part of a large dinner party meal or served simply on its own. When pomegranates are in season, sprinkle their lovely red seeds liberally over the salad.

BROCCOLI, CAULIFLOWER, FETA, COURGETTE AND CURRANT SALAD
FOR 6-8 AS A SIDE SALAD

½ head broccoli, separated into florets

½ head cauliflower, separated into florets

2 courgettes

2 tbsp extra virgin olive oil

4 tbsp pine nuts

4 tbsp currants or raisins

4 tbsp pomegranate molasses or lemon juice

1 bunch radishes, washed

200 g feta, cut into cubes

1 small handful mint leaves, shredded

4 spring onions, thinly sliced

salt and freshly ground black pepper

1. Steam or boil the broccoli until just cooked, then refresh in iced water and drain. Do the same with the cauliflower. Once they're both ready, put in a large bowl.

2. Top and tail the courgettes and slice 1 cm thick. Toss with 1 tbsp olive oil. Heat up a frying pan or griddle and cook on both sides until golden, then add to the broccoli and cauliflower.

3. Toast the pine nuts in the same pan with 1 tbsp olive oil until pale golden. Add the currants or raisins and cook over low heat until they swell up. Add the pomegranate molasses or lemon juice and bring to a sizzle, then pour over the vegetables.

4. Cut the radishes horizontally into thick slices and add to the vegetables along with the feta, mint and spring onions.

5. Toss everything together and taste for seasoning.

This dish can be served with vegetables or salad. Veal or beef mince can replace the lamb.

BAKED EGGPLANTS STUFFED WITH LAMB AND MOZZARELLA **FOR 4 MAIN COURSES**

3 eggplants
oil, for frying
1 red onion, peeled and thinly sliced
4 cloves garlic, peeled and sliced
2 bay leaves
½ tsp cumin seeds
5 cm cinnamon quill, snapped in half
1 tsp chilli flakes (more or less to taste)
2 tsp sumac (optional)
200 g minced lean lamb
1 x 400 g tin chopped tomatoes (or
   5 fresh tomatoes, diced)
2 tbsp soy sauce
100 ml water
salt and freshly ground black pepper
200 g mozzarella, sliced

1. Preheat oven to 180°C.

2. Split two of the eggplants in half lengthways, keeping the stalk intact. Using a small knife or soup spoon, scoop out their centres, leaving a 'shell' 1 cm thick. Place the shells in a roasting dish lined with baking paper.

3. Cut the stalk off the third eggplant and cut it into chunks along with the scooped-out flesh.

4. Fry the onion with the garlic and bay leaves until the onion begins to caramelize. Add the cumin seeds, cinnamon, chilli and sumac (if using) and fry for 1 minute, then add the minced lamb and diced eggplant.

5. As the mince cooks, use the back of a spoon to break it up and loosen it. Add the tomatoes, soy sauce and water and bring to the boil. Turn to a simmer and cook with a lid on for 20 minutes. Take the lid off, give it a stir and cook until most of the liquid has evaporated, stirring frequently. Taste for seasoning.

6. Spoon the mixture into the prepared eggplant halves and lay the mozzarella slices on top. Bake until the cheese has turned golden; around 15 minutes.

7. Serve straight away, although these are also lovely eaten the next day.

*Baking en papillote means 'in parchment' and it's a great way to steam-bake fish,
shellfish and poultry, although you could use it to cook anything. The key is to make
sure the package is sealed tightly so that no steam, and therefore juices or flavour, escape.*

CHICKEN BREAST EN PAPILLOTE WITH CHERRY TOMATOES AND ROSEMARY FOR 4 MAIN COURSES

4 chicken breasts (skin on or off)
salt and freshly ground black pepper
1 handful parsley leaves
1 tbsp fresh rosemary leaves, thyme,
    oregano or sage
4 cloves garlic, peeled and thinly sliced
2 tbsp olive oil
200 g cherry tomatoes

1. Preheat oven to 180°C.

2. Cut four pieces of baking paper approximately 30 cm square. Fold each one in half with the fold north–south, to produce a centre seam. Re-open the paper.

3. Season the chicken breasts and sprinkle with the parsley. Place one on each sheet of paper to the right of the centre seam.

4. Sauté the herbs and garlic over moderate heat in the olive oil until the garlic turns golden. Add the tomatoes and cook until around half of them have popped, shaking the pan from time to time. Spoon one-quarter of the tomatoes on top of each chicken breast, then drizzle with the pan juices.

5. Now the origami bit begins. Fold the left side of the paper over the breast and bring it flush to the right-hand side. Take the furthest end of the paper in your right hand, and put your forefinger next to the top of the breast. Fold the paper towards the right at a 90° angle. Twist and roll the right-hand edge of the package towards the bottom of the breast, to resemble a pasty, in order to seal it. Don't make it too tight as you need to allow some space for the steam to expand. Once the bag is twisted into a package, it's a good idea to tuck the final fold under itself to keep it sealed, or secure with a paper clip.

6. Place the packages on a baking tray and cook for 20 minutes. Take from the oven and leave to rest for 5 minutes. I like to serve the unopened package on the plate and give each guest a pair of scissors to cut their own open.

The texture of a soft goat's cheese (something like a French chèvre log) goes really well with the crunch of the pepitas (pumpkin seeds) and the fleshiness of the squash. Sunflower seeds or pecans can be used in place of the pepitas.

BUTTERNUT, GOAT'S CHEESE AND PEPITA SALAD **FOR 4–6 STARTERS**

1 butternut squash (about 600 g)
3 tbsp olive oil
1 tsp sweet smoked paprika or chilli flakes
60 g pepitas
salt and freshly ground black pepper
2 large handfuls rocket
3 tbsp lemon juice
200 g soft goat's cheese
2 tbsp capers

1. Preheat oven to 200°C.

2. Cut the top and bottom off the butternut, peel it and cut in half lengthways. Scoop the seeds out and discard. Slice it into 1 cm thick pieces.

3. Lay butternut on a baking tray lined with baking paper and brush 1 tbsp oil over each side. Season with salt and paprika or chilli, then bake until cooked.

4. While the butternut is cooking, heat up a pan with 2 tbsp oil and add the pepitas. Cook over a moderate heat, stirring often, until they're crisp, 3–4 minutes. They'll occasionally 'pop' but just keep stirring or shaking. Add a few pinches of salt to the pan, then tip them and the cooking oil (which will be a lovely green colour) into a small bowl to cool.

5. To serve, toss the rocket with the lemon juice and a little salt and pepper in a large bowl or on a platter. Sit the squash on and crumble the cheese over it. Scatter with the pepitas and capers. Serve warm or at room temperature.

You can grill the vegetables on a barbecue, under a grill in the oven or in a ridged skillet
pan. Whatever method you choose, they take on a lovely smoky flavour.

GRILLED VEGETABLE SALAD WITH FETA, HAZELNUTS, TOMATO AND BALSAMIC **FOR 6 STARTERS**

1 eggplant
olive oil
3 capsicums (red or yellow – avoid
  green as they're too bitter when
  cooked)
2 large courgettes
2 tomatoes
2 tbsp balsamic vinegar
salt and freshly ground black pepper
small handful basil leaves
200 g feta, roughly cut into cubes
60 g hazelnuts (almonds, pecans or
  walnuts are also good), toasted and
  chopped

1. Remove the stem from the eggplant and slice into ½ cm slices and brush with
olive oil.

2. Remove the stems from the capsicums, cut each into six wedges and flatten them
with your hand.

3. Cut both ends from the courgettes and cut each on an angle into at least nine
slices.

4. Toss the capsicums and courgettes with a few tablespoons of olive oil.

5. Grill the vegetables until coloured and tender, turning them to prevent burning.

6. Once the capsicums have blistered, place them in a plastic bag and leave to cool.

7. Dice the tomatoes and mix with 2 tbsp olive oil and the vinegar. Season well and
leave for 10 minutes.

8. To serve, toss the vegetables together with the basil and a little seasoning and
divide among your plates. Scatter the feta on top, spoon over the tomatoes and
sprinkle with the nuts.

A great first course or part of a buffet-style dinner, this salad is full of interesting textures and flavours with the rose-water adding a lovely twist. If you don't have any it'll still be a great salad.

ROAST CARROT, LENTIL AND HAZELNUT SALAD WITH ROSE-WATER
FOR 6 STARTERS

3 carrots, peeled or skins scrubbed

½ tsp coriander seeds

½ tsp cumin seeds

2 tsp balsamic vinegar

3 tbsp extra virgin olive oil

salt and freshly ground black pepper

100 g lentils, rinsed (green or Puy)

1 shallot or small red onion, peeled and
  chopped

2 bay leaves

1 tsp thyme leaves

150 g green beans, cut on an angle,
  blanched and refreshed

1 large handful olives

1 tbsp rose-water

1 tbsp lemon juice

2 handfuls salad leaves

100 g hazelnuts, toasted, skins rubbed
  off and crushed

1. Preheat oven to 180°C.

2. Cut both ends from the carrots, cut in half lengthways and slice into thick pieces. Put in a roasting dish with the coriander and cumin seeds, balsamic vinegar and 1 tbsp olive oil and toss it all together. Lightly season and roast until they begin to colour and soften a little, stirring a couple of times. They'll take around 30 minutes. Once cooked, tip into a bowl with all the pan juices.

3. Put the lentils, shallot or onion, bay leaves, thyme and 1 tbsp olive oil in a pot and add enough cold water to cover by 2 cm. Bring to the boil, then rapidly simmer until the lentils are cooked, 15–25 minutes, stirring occasionally. If they look a little dry, top up with a little hot water. Leave to cool, then season with salt and pepper.

4. To serve, mix the beans and olives with the carrots, rose-water and lemon juice and remaining olive oil. Gently mix in the salad leaves and divide among your plates. Spoon the lentils on and scatter with the hazelnuts.

The hero of this dish is the tea-eggs because they're incredibly beautiful. I remember watching a TV show, as a 10-year-old, where they showed how these are created in China – I was mesmerized. Any dark tea will give the desired look, but lapsang souchong will also give a delicious smoky flavour.

ASPARAGUS, ROCKET AND ALMOND SALAD WITH TEA-EGGS **FOR 4 STARTERS**

4 eggs
1 tbsp lapsang souchong tea leaves
6 tbsp soy sauce
400 g asparagus
1 tbsp cider vinegar or lemon juice
1 tbsp runny honey
1 tsp finely grated ginger
3 tbsp extra virgin olive oil
salt and freshly ground black pepper
2 handfuls rocket leaves
80 g flaked almonds, toasted

1. Place the eggs in a pot of boiling water and cook for 4 minutes. Drain and refresh in cold water until cool enough to handle.

2. Holding one egg at a time, use a spoon to gently smash the shell – the more cracks you have, the more the flavour and colour will get in. Place back in the pot and add enough cold water to cover by 2 cm. Add the tea leaves and 5 tbsp soy and bring to a boil. Turn to a rapid simmer and cook with the lid on for 30 minutes. Leave to cool in the liquor for 1 hour, or overnight, then peel.

3. Snap the woody stem end from the asparagus and discard. Steam or boil spears for a few minutes, then refresh in cold water. Cut each spear into three on an angle.

4. Stir the vinegar or lemon juice, reserved soy, honey and ginger together, then mix in the olive oil and season.

5. To serve, toss the rocket leaves with the asparagus and almonds and divide among four plates. Cut the eggs in half and sit them on top, then drizzle with the dressing.

Oily fish are terrific cooked this way, as they become slightly caramelized and very juicy.
You could use tuna, scallops or prawns instead of salmon. Soaking the wooden skewers
in water prevents them burning.

SALMON TERIYAKI SKEWERS WITH NOODLE SALAD **FOR 4 STARTERS**

600 g salmon fillet, from the fattest end,
  skin and bones removed
125 ml soy sauce (use one that's not too
  dark and salty – if it is, dilute with
  water)
2 tbsp mirin (or 1 tbsp caster sugar)
1 tbsp finely chopped ginger
2 tsp sesame oil
8 bamboo skewers
80 g dried green tea noodles or soba
  noodles (or any Asian-style noodle)
2 tsp sesame seeds, toasted
1 spring onion, thinly sliced
vegetable oil

1. Cut the salmon into fat, even-sized cubes.

2. Reserve 1 tbsp soy sauce, then place the remainder in a bowl and mix with the mirin (or sugar), ginger and sesame oil.

3. Add the salmon and gently mix together, then place in the fridge, covered, for 2 hours. Mix gently a few times while it's marinating.

4. Soak 8 bamboo skewers in warm water for 1 hour.

5. Cook the noodles in plenty of lightly salted, gently boiling water until al dente. Drain and rinse with cold water. Toss with the reserved soy sauce, the sesame seeds and spring onion.

6. When it's ready, take the salmon from the marinade and poke onto the skewers. Brush the skewers with the vegetable oil and grill for no more than 20 seconds on each side, at which point the salmon will be still quite rare, but juicy and succulent.

7. To serve, pile the noodle salad on your plates and sit two skewers on top of each.

These skewers take their inspiration from the various summer holidays I've had sailing around Turkey and the Greek islands. Yellowfin tuna works a treat, as does sustainable swordfish – it pays to know how well sourced your fish is. Otherwise, use monkfish or salmon, scallops or prawns.

TUNA SKEWERS AND SQUID WITH PARSLEY YOGHURT

FOR 4 STARTERS

500 g tuna, cut into 2 cm dice
2 tsp fresh thyme or oregano leaves
2 cloves garlic, peeled and sliced
4 tbsp olive oil
1 lemon (plus some wedges to serve)
400 g small squid, the legs and bodies
   separated, gutted
sea salt and freshly ground black
   pepper
8 bamboo skewers
½ cup plain Greek-style yoghurt
1 small handful shredded flat parsley
   leaves

1. Place the tuna, herbs, garlic and half the olive oil in a bowl and gently mix.

2. Finely grate ½ tsp lemon zest and add to the fish.

3. Cut the squid heads into 1 cm rings and add to the bowl along with the legs. Toss it all together with a little sea salt and pepper. Cover and keep chilled for 1 hour.

4. Soak 8 bamboo skewers in warm water for 1 hour.

5. While the fish is marinating, mix 1 tbsp of the remaining oil into the yoghurt along with the parsley and a squeeze of lemon juice, then cover and place in the fridge.

6. Thread the tuna onto your skewers, brushing each one with the remaining oil.

7. Heat up a pan or skillet, and when smoking place the skewers in. Cook for no more than 15 seconds on each side, as tuna is lovely eaten medium-rare.

8. Take the skewers out of the pan and add the marinating squid while the pan is still fairly hot. Cook, for 30–45 seconds only, stirring and shaking the pan. Squid toughens when overcooked, so keep an eye on it.

9. To serve, simply place the skewers and squid together on a plate and serve the yoghurt either in a separate bowl or dollop it on top. Serve with lemon wedges.

These capsicums remind me of Mediterranean summers because around the Med stuffed
vegetables are commonplace, whether tomatoes, capsicums, courgettes or eggplants.
Serve two per person for a main course, or one as part of a barbecue buffet meal. They
can be eaten straight away, but they're even better eaten at room temperature the next
day drizzled with a little more olive oil and lemon juice.

BAKED CAPSICUMS STUFFED WITH BASMATI RICE AND LAMB FOR 4 MAIN COURSES

2 red onions, peeled and thinly sliced
2 tbsp olive oil
6 cloves garlic, peeled and chopped
1 red chilli, chopped (or chilli flakes, to
   taste)
2 tsp cumin seeds
3 tbsp rosemary leaves
200 g minced lean lamb
2 tomatoes, roughly chopped
2 pinches saffron
200 ml red wine
100 g basmati rice (or any other rice)
salt and freshly ground black pepper
8 red or yellow capsicums
1 handful mint leaves
boiling water

1. Preheat oven to 180°C. Line a deep-sided roasting dish with baking paper – it needs to be able to hold all 8 capsicums comfortably.

2. In a medium saucepan, sauté the onions in the olive oil until beginning to caramelize. Stir in the garlic, chilli, cumin and 1 tbsp rosemary and continue to cook for another 3–4 minutes, stirring frequently.

3. Add the minced lamb and tomatoes and stir, making sure the mince breaks up.

4. Add the saffron and wine and bring to the boil.

5. Stir in the rice and 1 tsp salt and bring back to the boil. Put a lid on the pan and cook over a rapid simmer for 12 minutes.

6. Using a small sharp knife, cut the tops off the capsicums, keeping them and their stalks intact. Use your fingers to pull the seeds out. Scatter the remaining rosemary in the roasting dish.

7. Once the lamb is ready, stir in the mint and taste for seasoning. Spoon the mixture into the capsicums — allow a little room for expansion. Put the tops back on the capsicums and place them upright in the roasting dish, then pour in a cup of boiling water. Cover loosely with foil and bake for 20 minutes, then take the foil off and continue to cook until they begin to colour and soften.

This is a vegetarian version of a Thai beef salad (well, not really as it contains fish sauce, but you get the idea). The squash works really well with the sharp chillied dressing, and the crunch of the peanuts adds a lovely textural quality.

WARM SALAD OF ROAST SQUASH AND GARLIC WITH PEANUTS AND LIME CHILLI DRESSING FOR 4 STARTERS

500 g squash or pumpkin

8 cloves garlic, peeled and halved lengthways (more or less to taste)

salt

50 ml extra virgin olive oil

4 tsp hot water

4 tbsp lime or lemon juice

½ tsp finely grated lime or lemon zest

1 red chilli, finely chopped (more or less to taste)

2 tsp fish sauce or soy sauce (or a little salt)

2 tsp grated palm sugar or brown sugar

100 g peanuts, roasted and crushed

1 small handful picked coriander leaves

1. Preheat oven to 200°C.

2. Cut the squash or pumpkin into chunks, removing the seeds. You can roast it with the skin on, as it's edible, but you may prefer to remove it.

3. Place the squash in a baking paper-lined roasting dish. Scatter the garlic, season with salt, drizzle on the oil and pour on the hot water.

4. Roast for about 30 minutes until cooked, depending on the thickness of the flesh.

5. While it's cooking, mix the lime or lemon juice and zest with the chilli, fish sauce or soy and sugar until the sugar has dissolved.

6. To serve, divide the squash, garlic and roasting juices among your plates. Sprinkle on the peanuts, pour on the dressing and scatter with the coriander.

I'm a huge fan of smoked fish and so this to me is perfect comfort food. However, it's also really tasty made with shredded ham or smoked turkey.

SMOKED FISH, POTATO, FETA AND BROCCOLI TART

FOR 6 MAIN COURSES OR 8 STARTERS

350 g puff pastry
a little butter
300 g boiling potatoes, peeled and
  roughly cut into 1 cm cubes
½ head broccoli, blanched then roughly
  chopped, keeping smaller florets
  whole
1 handful parsley, roughly chopped
150 g smoked fish, skin and bones
  removed, flaked
100 g feta cheese, crumbled
2 eggs, lightly beaten
salt and freshly ground black pepper
watercress or rocket, to serve

1. Preheat oven to 200°C.

2. Roll the pastry out to just less than ½ cm thick and line a buttered 24 cm fluted tart tin with it, reserving the trimmings. Place in the fridge while you make the filling. Roll the trimmings out to make a rectangle roughly 25 cm long and place in the fridge to firm up.

3. Boil the potatoes in lightly salted water until cooked, then drain and leave to cool for 5 minutes on a tray. Place in a bowl and gently toss with the broccoli, parsley, smoked fish, feta and three-quarters of the beaten egg, seasoning with pepper and just a little salt.

4. Spoon the filling into the pastry case and smooth the top. Take the rectangular piece of rolled-out trimmings and cut lengthways into roughly 6 mm-wide strips. Lay these lattice-style over the tart, pressing them into the edge of the pastry to hold them in place. Brush with the reserved beaten egg and bake in the lower part of the oven until the pastry is golden and slightly puffed; around 30–40 minutes.

5. Take from the oven and leave to rest for 15 minutes before removing from the tin.

6. To serve, all you really need is a peppery leaf salad like watercress or rocket. The tart is also lovely eaten cold the next day.

*There's nothing more casual than serving guests a bowl of shellfish that you eat with
your fingers. Remember to have finger bowls of warm water with sliced lemon in it on
the table. This dish can be made with just mussels, or a combination of clams, cockles,
mussels, etc. – it's up to you. Just make sure the shellfish are well washed and purged of
any sand, as grit will ruin your meal.*

COCKLES AND MUSSELS WITH TOMATO, CHILLI AND MINT

FOR 6-8 STARTERS

1 large red onion, peeled, halved and
  thinly sliced

1 red chilli, sliced

4 cloves garlic, peeled and thinly sliced

1 tbsp olive oil

2 pinches saffron (optional – but it adds
  a lovely complexity)

1 kg cockles or clams

1 kg mussels, beards and barnacles
  removed

3 large tomatoes, diced

1 glass white wine (nothing too sweet)

50 g butter

1 small handful mint leaves, shredded

1. In a large pot sauté the onion, chilli and garlic in the oil until beginning to
caramelize, stirring well so it doesn't catch.

2. Add the saffron (if using), then the shellfish. Turn the heat to full and put the lid
on. Cook for 2 minutes, shaking the pan from side to side every now and then.

3. Give it a good stir and add the tomatoes, wine and butter, then put the lid back on.

4. Cook until all the shellfish have opened, 3–4 minutes, giving them a stir from
time to time. Any that haven't opened at this point should be discarded.

5. To serve, stir in the mint then ladle into bowls.

| CHAPTER FIVE |

DINNER

You can use any steak for this; whilst rump might not be the most tender cut, it certainly makes up for it in flavour.

RUMP STEAK ON SWEDE AND PARSNIP MASH WITH BEETROOT SALSA **FOR 4 MAIN COURSES**

4 rump steaks, each 140–180 g

salt and freshly ground black pepper

350 g parsnips, peeled and cut into chunks

350 g swedes, peeled and cut into chunks

1 heaped tbsp rosemary leaves, roughly chopped

80 g butter

1 handful parsley, roughly chopped

1 medium beetroot, roasted or boiled until cooked, peeled and coarsely grated

½ tsp caraway seeds, cumin seeds or coriander seeds (optional but delicious)

2 tbsp olive oil, plus extra for brushing

2 tbsp balsamic vinegar

300 g spinach, washed and drained

1. Lightly season the steak and leave it to come to room temperature.

2. Boil the parsnips and swedes with half the rosemary in lightly salted water. Once cooked, drain in a colander and return to the pot.

3. Cook the butter over medium heat to a nut-brown colour, stirring it a little as it colours, then mash this into the root vegetables along with the parsley and keep warm.

4. Place the grated beetroot in a bowl.

5. Sauté the remaining rosemary and the seeds (if using) in a pan with the olive oil until the rosemary sizzles. Pour over the beetroot and mix in the balsamic vinegar. Season with salt and pepper.

6. Steam or sauté the spinach to wilt it, then drain in a colander and keep warm.

7. Heat up a skillet, grill or heavy pan and brush the steaks with olive oil. Cook over a medium-high heat until cooked to your preferred stage. I cook mine for 5 minutes, then turn over and cook for another 2–3 minutes depending on the thickness of the meat. Take the steaks off the heat, place on a warm plate and let them rest for 4–5 minutes, which will keep the meat juicy.

8. To serve, divide the mash and spinach between four warmed plates. Slice the steak into fat fingers and sit them on top, then spoon on the beetroot salsa.

Fish cooked on the bone retains moisture, much like a meat chop or roast leg of lamb. Do look out for bones, though, and make sure the fish has had its scales removed.

SNAPPER STEAKS WITH CAPER AND OLIVE SALAD **FOR 4 MAIN COURSES**

3 tbsp extra virgin olive oil

6 cloves garlic, peeled and sliced

1 handful flat parsley, leaves picked (save the stalks)

4 x 200 g snapper steaks (cut from a fish that has been gutted and scaled)

1 tsp sweet smoked paprika

salt

150 ml white wine (pinot gris, sauvignon blanc or dry riesling would be a good match)

2 tbsp capers (rinse if they're in a strong brine or vinegar)

100 g assorted olives (pitted if you want)

1. Brush 1 tbsp oil on the bottom of a roasting dish just large enough to hold the fish comfortably, and put half the garlic and all of the parsley stalks in.

2. Dust the fish on both sides with the paprika and a little salt and place in the dish.

3. Scatter the remaining garlic on the steaks, then drizzle with the wine and another tablespoon of oil.

4. Cover the dish and leave to sit at room temperature for 1 hour.

5. Preheat oven to 160°C.

6. Remove the cover, turn the fish over and place in the oven. Bake until the snapper is just cooked – pry the flesh back at the thickest point next to the bones; it should be opaque rather than raw. It will take 20–30 minutes, depending on the thickness of the fish.

7. Mix the capers with the olives, parsley leaves and remaining 1 tbsp olive oil.

8. To serve, put the steaks on warm plates. Remove the parsley stalks from the roasting dish, then pour the roasting juices over and spoon on the capers and olives.

Any thick meaty fish will work cooked this way – just avoid oily fish as they'll be too rich. Serve with noodles or mash, steamed greens and minted peas.

COD POACHED IN CREAMY LEEKS, GINGER AND SAFFRON **FOR 4 MAIN COURSES**

800 g cod fillet, skin and bones
   removed, cut into 4
salt and freshly ground black pepper
2 tbsp cornflour or plain flour
50 g butter
1 small leek, rinsed and very finely
   sliced
1 pinch saffron threads
1 tsp peeled and finely chopped ginger
300 ml light fish stock
150 ml cream

1. Season the cod on both sides and dust with cornflour or flour.

2. Choose a pan that will hold the fish comfortably, with a tight-fitting lid, and place on medium-low heat.

3. Add the butter, then when it's sizzling add the leek, saffron and ginger. Cook until wilted, stirring occasionally.

4. Add the fish stock and bring to the boil, then reduce to a rapid simmer and cook for 5 minutes.

5. Add the cream and cook until bubbling, then tuck the fish in.

6. Reduce to a simmer, and put a lid on. After 5 minutes, gently turn the fish over and see how cooked it is. A piece of cod 3 cm thick should take about 10 minutes to cook.

7. When it's done, carefully remove the fish from the pan and place on four warmed plates. Bring the sauce back to a gentle boil and cook to reduce the sauce to a thick, creamy consistency. Taste for seasoning, then spoon the leeks and sauce over the fish.

Serve this dish with white rice: either jasmine or basmati. You can add sliced dried apricots or mango, or lightly toasted desiccated coconut to the curry as it's cooking.

CHICKEN MACADAMIA CURRY
WITH BANANA RAITA **FOR 4-6 MAIN COURSES**

1 large chicken (or 4 boneless legs and
  2 breasts)
6 green cardamoms, crushed
6 star anise
1 x 10 cm piece cassia or cinnamon
  quill, snapped into 3–4 pieces
1 red chilli, chopped (more or less to
  taste)
1 thumb ginger, peeled and grated
2 tbsp sesame oil
3 spring onions
80 g macadamia nuts, toasted and
  roughly chopped
400 ml unsweetened coconut milk
1 tbsp fish sauce (or soy sauce or salt, to
  taste)
hot water
salt and freshly ground black pepper
1 banana
juice of ½ lemon
200 ml plain Greek-style yoghurt
1 small handful mint and coriander,
  shredded

1. At least 4 hours (and up to 12 hours) before you're planning to eat, prepare the chicken. Remove the bones and skin. Cut the leg meat roughly into 1 cm thick slices and the breast meat into 2 cm slices. Place in a mixing bowl with the spices, chilli, ginger and sesame oil.

2. Thinly slice the green tops of the spring onions and reserve. Cut the remainder into 3 cm lengths and add to the chicken. Toss it all together, cover tightly and place in the fridge to marinate for 4–12 hours.

3. When the chicken is ready, heat up a large saucepan. Add half the chicken and its marinade then brown it all over, being careful not to burn it. Take it out and cook the other half.

4. Return the first batch to the pan with the macadamias, coconut milk and fish sauce (or soy or salt), then enough hot water to almost cover the meat. Bring to a boil, then turn to a simmer and cook for 8–10 minutes until the chicken is cooked through, stirring several times.

5. Taste for seasoning and adjust if necessary.

6. While the curry is cooking, peel and dice the banana and mix with the lemon juice. Mix in the yoghurt, the reserved spring onion tops, mint and coriander, and season.

7. To serve, divide the curry among warmed bowls and spoon the raita on top.

Salmon is one fish that should never be cooked more than medium-rare. In my restaurants we cook salmon rare then rest it for 10 minutes or so before serving, ensuring a tender and translucent fish that's very succulent.

CRISPY-SKIN SALMON ON THYME POTATOES WITH BEANS AND LEMON DRESSING FOR 4 MAIN COURSES

4 x 160 g pieces salmon fillet, bones removed, scaled if you prefer

sea salt and freshly ground black pepper

100 g unsalted butter, melted

500 g small waxy potatoes

1 tsp fresh thyme

2 handfuls green beans, topped and tailed

2 tbsp lemon juice

2 tbsp lemon-scented extra virgin olive oil or best-quality extra virgin olive oil

picked parsley, to garnish

1. Preheat oven to 180°C.

2. Lightly season the fish on both sides and leave to come to room temperature.

3. Brush a roasting dish with 1 tbsp butter.

4. Boil the potatoes in salted water for 10 minutes, then drain and slice in half lengthways. Put in the roasting dish with the thyme, half the remaining butter, and some sea salt and pepper. Roast until done, 15–20 minutes, tossing the potatoes occasionally.

5. When the potatoes are almost ready, heat up a heavy-based pan and add the remaining butter. Sit the fish in, skin-side down, and cook over a moderate heat without moving for about 8 minutes. Because the fish cooks from the skin-side upwards, it pays to baste it. Just tilt the pan every few minutes, keeping it on the heat, and use a spoon to scoop up some of the pan juices and drizzle over the fish.

6. When the flesh becomes opaque towards the top, the fleshy side, turn the heat off.

7. Meanwhile, cook the beans, then drain and mix with the roast potatoes.

8. To serve, divide the vegetables among four plates and sit a piece of salmon on top. Mix the lemon juice and oil together and spoon over the fish, then scatter with the parsley.

Verjus is a terrific ingredient. Slightly acidic but not as sour as vinegar, it goes really well with white meat and fish or in salad dressings. If you can't get verjus, use half lemon juice or cider vinegar and half water. Use a firm white fish for this dish, such as cod, hapuku (New Zealand), halibut or John Dory – cooking times will depend on the thickness of the fish.

BAKED FISH ON TOMATO GINGER SALAD WITH PINE NUT SAUCE
FOR 4 MAIN COURSES

4 x 180 g pieces thick fish fillet, skin and
  bones removed
1 handful basil leaves, roughly torn
1 red chilli, sliced (more or less to taste)
3 tbsp extra virgin olive oil
100 g pine nuts, lightly toasted
1 tsp flaky sea salt
120 ml verjus
1 tsp finely grated, peeled ginger
1 clove garlic, peeled and grated
6 ripe tomatoes, sliced
2 tbsp snipped chives
8 mint leaves, shredded
salt and freshly ground black pepper

1. Place the fish in a non-reactive roasting dish, just large enough to hold it all comfortably without being crammed.

2. Mix the basil, chilli, oil, pine nuts and flaky sea salt together and rub it all over the fish. Leave to marinate for 1 hour, sealed tightly with plastic wrap.

3. Preheat oven to 180°C.

4. Pour half the verjus over the fish and roast until almost cooked through; about 6–10 minutes. Take from the oven and leave in a warm place for 2 minutes.

5. While the fish is cooking, mix the reserved verjus with the ginger and garlic then toss with the tomatoes, chives and mint and lightly season.

6. To serve, divide the tomato salad among four plates and sit a piece of fish on each. Give the roasting pan ingredients a good mix, then spoon over and around the fish.

This warming winter dish will go with most starches, from rice and couscous through to noodles or mash. Add some steamed greens and you've got a meal.

WHISKY-BRAISED PORK BELLY WITH SHIITAKE MUSHROOMS AND STAR ANISE **FOR 6 MAIN COURSES**

1 kg pork belly, bones and skin removed
80 ml whisky (or sherry or dark rum)
12 dried or fresh shiitake mushrooms
2 red onions, peeled and thickly sliced
2 tbsp vegetable oil
2 tsp sesame oil
3 carrots, peeled and thickly sliced
12 cloves garlic, peeled and roughly
    chopped
2 thumbs ginger, peeled and thinly
    sliced
8 star anise
6 cloves
4 tbsp soy sauce, plus a little extra
2 tbsp honey
hot water
1 tbsp cornflour
4 tbsp cold water
salt and freshly ground black pepper

1. Preheat oven to 180°C.

2. Cut the belly into large chunks (about 3 cm square), mix with the whisky and leave to marinate for 4 hours.

3. Soak the mushrooms (if using dried) in 500 ml warm water for 1 hour. Once done, cut their stalks off and discard. Keep the soaking liquor.

4. Heat up a large heavy-based ovenproof pot and sauté the onions in the vegetable oil and sesame oil until caramelized.

5. Add the carrots, garlic, ginger, spices, soy sauce and honey, along with the mushrooms (and soaking liquor if using dried), and bring to the boil.

6. Stir in the belly and whisky and pour on enough hot water to just cover the meat. Bring back to the boil.

7. Cover the pot tightly with a lid (or foil) and cook for 2 hours. Take from the oven.

8. Dissolve the cornflour in the cold water and stir it into the braise. Simmer on the stove for a minute.

9. Taste for seasoning, adding extra soy sauce or salt.

I enjoy serving a whole roast fish as the main course at a dinner party, getting people to pass it around on a platter as they help themselves. A whole John Dory or snapper, or several trout, work well cooked this way.

ROAST JOHN DORY, PEANUTS, CHILLI AND CORIANDER WITH COCONUT DRESSING **FOR 4-6 MAIN COURSES**

1.5–2 kg whole fish, gutted, all sharp fins cut off with scissors, scales removed

salt and freshly ground black pepper

1 red chilli, finely chopped (more or less to taste)

2 cloves garlic, peeled and thinly sliced

1 thumb ginger, peeled and thinly chopped

60 g peanuts, roasted and chopped

1 small bunch coriander, roots included, shredded

1 tbsp sesame oil

400 ml unsweetened coconut milk

2 tbsp fish sauce

1 tsp finely grated lime zest

2 tbsp lime juice

1. Rinse the fish inside and out and pat dry with kitchen paper. Slash the skin on both sides in three places, 2 cm apart, from the dorsal fin (the top) to the stomach (the lower edge of the fish). Season inside and out.

2. Mix the chilli, garlic, ginger, peanuts and half the coriander together.

3. Take a piece of foil, three times the length of the fish. Lay a piece of baking paper on top, and brush with the sesame oil. Scatter one-third of the peanut mixture in the centre of the baking paper. Lay the fish on top and put another one-third of the peanut mixture in the stomach cavity. Sprinkle the remaining mixture on the fish.

4. Fold the foil over the fish and wrap it up, sealing tightly. Place in a large roasting dish or similar and leave to infuse for 1–4 hours, turning over halfway through.

5. You can cook this over the glowing coals of a barbecue or in an oven set at 170°C. It will take 40–60 minutes, depending on the thickness of the fish. Cook for 30 minutes, turn over and after another 10 minutes cut a slash in the foil, near the head end, and check how it's doing. The flesh should be almost cooked and opaque.

6. While it's roasting, put the coconut milk, fish sauce, lime zest and juice in a pan. Bring to a gentle boil, then reduce the heat to a simmer and cook until thickened, around 10 minutes.

7. To serve, transfer the fish to a platter along with the peanut mixture and scatter the reserved coriander on top. Either pour the sauce over or serve in a jug.

An aromatic stew, the chicken is best cooked on the bone to keep it juicy, although boneless thighs will also work. Try replacing the chicken with chunks of thick fish fillet, and the beans can be replaced with asparagus in season.

CHICKEN AND PEANUT COCONUT CURRY **FOR 4 MAIN COURSES**

8 chicken thighs, bone in, skin on

vegetable oil

2 red onions, peeled and thinly sliced

6 cloves garlic, peeled and roughly chopped

1 green chilli, sliced into rings (more or less to taste)

1 tsp fennel seeds

10 cm cinnamon quill, snapped in half

4 star anise

2 tbsp grated dark palm sugar or brown sugar

2 tbsp fish sauce or soy sauce

400 ml unsweetened coconut milk

400 ml water

50 g roasted peanuts, roughly chopped

12 baby corn

100 g green beans or asparagus, briefly blanched and refreshed

salt and freshly ground black pepper

rice or noodles, to serve

coriander, to garnish

1. Sauté the chicken in 1 tbsp oil until golden brown all over. Take from the pan and put on a plate.

2. Put the pan back on the heat (no need to clean it out) and caramelize the onions, garlic and chilli.

3. Add the spices, sugar and fish sauce or soy sauce and bring to a boil. Cook to evaporate the sauce until thick.

4. Add the coconut milk and water. Bring to a boil, then simmer for 5 minutes.

5. Return the chicken to the pan. Add the peanuts and bring back to a boil, then turn to a rapid simmer and put a lid on.

6. After 10 minutes turn the chicken thighs over and continue cooking. They'll take around 20 minutes in total.

7. While the chicken is cooking, heat a frying pan until very hot. Add 1 tsp oil and then the corn. Cook over a medium-high heat until golden all over.

8. Once the chicken is cooked, mix in the corn and beans, then take off the heat. Taste for seasoning.

9. Serve with plain rice or noodles and sprinkle with coriander sprigs.

This is a great summer salad, when the lamb is a little fatter than in early spring and cherries are in season. Surprisingly, cherries and new potatoes go really well together. A chump, or rump, is best cooked medium as any less will be a bit chewy. This can be served cold or at room temperature.

LAMB ON CHERRY POTATO SALAD
FOR 4 MAIN COURSES

4 x 160 g lamb rumps (or any other prime cut), trimmed
2 tbsp olive oil
300 g new potatoes
1 red onion, peeled and sliced
6 cloves garlic, peeled and sliced
2 tsp oregano or thyme leaves (or a mixture of both)
16 cherries, pitted and halved
salt and freshly ground black pepper
2 tbsp balsamic or red wine vinegar
2 handfuls salad leaves

1. Preheat oven to 180°C. Place a roasting dish on the middle shelf of the oven.

2. Score the lamb fat. Place a frying pan over medium heat, add 1 tsp oil, then place the lamb in, fat-side down. Cook over a moderate heat for 5 minutes to render some of the fat from the rumps and give a lovely colour.

3. Turn the rumps over and transfer to the roasting dish, then put in the oven. Roast for 13–15 minutes for medium-cooked.

4. Turn the oven off and leave the door open while you rest the meat and finish the dish.

5. Boil the potatoes in salted water until cooked, then drain and cut in half if small, or slice 1 cm thick.

6. Caramelize the onion and garlic over medium heat in the remaining oil, stirring often. Add the potatoes, herbs and cherries and continue to cook so that it's all warmed through. Season, mix in the vinegar, then take off the heat.

7. To serve, divide the potato salad among four warm plates and scatter with the salad leaves. Slice the lamb against the grain and lay on top.

Marinating less-tender cuts of meat in a yoghurt-based marinade is very much a Tandoori technique – the enzymes in the yoghurt help to tenderize the meat. Serve this as it is with a cucumber and mint salad or thinly sliced tomatoes mixed with coriander and grated ginger.

TANDOORI-STYLE CHICKEN WITH SAFFRON LEMON RICE **FOR 4 MAIN COURSES**

4 large chicken legs (thigh and drumstick)

300 ml plain yoghurt

3 tbsp vegetable oil

4 cloves garlic, peeled and chopped

2 tbsp rosemary leaves

2 tsp smoked paprika or regular paprika

1 tsp cumin seeds or fennel seeds

1 tsp flaky salt

300 g basmati or jasmine rice

1 pinch saffron (it's a surprisingly strong spice so use sparingly)

3 strips lemon peel

½ tsp salt

550 ml cold water

1 handful coriander leaves, to garnish

1 lemon, quartered

1. Cut the legs in half at the joint and remove the knuckle, if still attached.

2. In a bowl, mix together the yoghurt, oil, garlic, rosemary, paprika, cumin or fennel seeds and flaky salt. Add the chicken and toss it all together, making sure the marinade coats the chicken evenly. Cover tightly and put in the fridge for between 2 and 12 hours. The longer it marinates, the tastier and more tender it will be.

3. Preheat oven to 190°C. Line a roasting tray with baking paper (it'll make it easier to clean) and sit the chicken pieces on it. Roast for 30–40 minutes, turning them over halfway through, until cooked. To test, cut through the thickest part of the thigh with a small knife – the juices should run out clear.

4. While the chicken is roasting, cook the rice. Rinse it in a sieve under cold running water, then put in a pot. Add the saffron, lemon peel, salt and cold water. Bring to the boil, then turn to a simmer, put the lid on and cook for 10 minutes. Turn the heat off and leave to sit in a warm place undisturbed until the chicken is cooked.

5. To serve, divide the rice among four plates and sit the chicken and any roasting juices on top. Garnish with the coriander and serve with a lemon wedge.

Very rich yet also very refreshing, this curry can be served as a meal on its own or as the vegetable component of a main course. Pumpkin, celeriac and even potatoes can be used instead of the butternut. Serve with steamed rice or couscous.

RED CURRIED BUTTERNUT, MUSHROOMS AND SPINACH
FOR 4-6 MAIN COURSES

1 kg butternut squash, peeled, deseeded and cut into large chunks

4 green cardamoms (or ⅛ tsp ground cardamom or ground cinnamon)

2 red capsicums, quartered and deseeded

3 tomatoes, quartered

1 red chilli (more or less to taste)

3 cloves garlic, peeled

1 thumb ginger, peeled and sliced

3 tbsp tomato paste

½ tsp salt

4 tbsp water

1 tbsp vegetable oil

6 portobello mushrooms, quartered

400 g spinach, washed and stalks removed

250 ml plain yoghurt

coriander, to garnish

1. Boil or steam the butternut until it's only half cooked – it should have some resistance when pushing a knife through to test it.

2. Bash the cardamoms and pull the seeds out from the green husks. It might seem fiddly but the flavour is worth it.

3. Purée the capsicums, tomatoes, chilli, garlic, ginger and tomato paste in a blender with the salt and water.

4. Pour the purée into a wide pan with the cardamom seeds (or ground cardamom or cinnamon) and oil and bring to the boil, stirring frequently. It will 'plop' a bit so keep stirring it slowly. Cook for 1 minute.

5. Once it's warmed up, stir in the butternut. Put a lid on the pan and simmer until the butternut is just about cooked.

6. Gently stir in the mushrooms and cook for 2 minutes.

7. Lastly, stir in the spinach until it wilts, then mix in the yoghurt and take off the heat. Garnish with coriander to finish.

This open-top pie is rather like a quiche. The 'mushroom custard' on top hides the juicy chicken filling beneath. You could serve it hot, but I prefer it at room temperature, and it's just as good served the next day. Serve with either a green salad or steamed veggies.

CREAMY CHICKEN, MUSHROOM AND PARSNIP PIE FOR 6–8 MAIN COURSES

250 g short crust pastry (see page 176)
1 onion, peeled and thinly sliced
4 cloves garlic, peeled and sliced
50 g butter (or 2 tbsp olive oil)
2 parsnips, peeled, cores removed if
    woody, then roughly cut into 1 cm
    dice
500 g chicken mince
200 ml water
flaky salt and freshly ground black
    pepper
400 g open-capped mushrooms
    (portobello mushrooms look best)
3 eggs
200 ml cream
2 tbsp snipped chives

1. Preheat oven to 180°C.

2. Roll pastry out roughly to a 32 cm disc, 5 mm thick. Line a 24 cm diameter tart tin with the pastry and place in the fridge for 20 minutes to firm up.

3. Line the pastry with baking paper, three-quarters fill with baking beans or rice and blind bake for 15 minutes. Cool for a few minutes, then remove the paper and beans. Reduce the oven temperature to 170°C.

4. While the pastry is cooking, make the filling. Sauté the onion and garlic in the butter or oil until the onion begins to caramelize, stirring occasionally.

5. Stir in the parsnip and cook a few minutes more.

6. Stir in the mince, breaking it up as it cooks, until lightly coloured.

7. Add the water, 1 tsp flaky salt and plenty of pepper and bring to the boil. Reduce the heat to a rapid simmer and cook until the liquid has almost evaporated, stirring frequently.

8. Slice the mushrooms 5 mm thick and reserve the 15 best slices. Once the liquid has evaporated from the chicken, stir in the mushrooms.

9. Beat 2 eggs with the cream and season with ½ tsp flaky salt. Mix half of this into the chicken, along with the third egg, and spoon into the pastry case, pressing it flat.

10. Gently pour the remaining creamy mixture on top and scatter with the reserved sliced mushrooms and the chives.

11. Bake until the custard has set, 25–30 minutes. Take from the oven and leave to cool in the tin.

QUICK FOOD-PROCESSOR SHORT CRUST PASTRY MAKES 300 g

180 g flour
1 pinch salt
90 g chilled unsalted butter, cut into
   1 cm chunks
1 large egg yolk
3 tsp cold water
1 tbsp extra virgin olive oil

1. Place the flour and salt in a food processor and blitz for 5 seconds. Add the butter and pulse until it resembles breadcrumbs.

2. Beat the egg yolk with cold water and add to the processor with the oil. Pulse until it just holds together.

3. Tip onto a bench and gently knead until it forms a dough, being careful not to overwork it as it will toughen.

4. Wrap in plastic wrap and place in the fridge until needed.

This is what I call a summer curry – simple to make, light and fresh. You can pick up a good brand of Thai green curry paste from South-East Asian stores and some supermarkets and delis.

SNAPPER ON VEGGIE COCONUT CURRY WITH TOMATO SALSA

FOR 4 MAIN COURSES

2 small red onions, peeled

2 tomatoes, diced

1 spring onion, thinly sliced

2 tbsp extra virgin olive oil

1 tbsp red or white vinegar

salt and freshly ground black pepper

2 tbsp vegetable oil

2 tsp Thai green curry paste (more or less to taste)

400 ml unsweetened coconut milk

1 tbsp fish sauce (or soy sauce or salt, to taste)

2 carrots, peeled and thinly sliced

1 courgette, ends removed, thinly sliced

½ bunch asparagus, ends snapped off and discarded, cut into 3 cm lengths

750 g fish fillet, bones removed, cut into 4 pieces

1. Make the salsa. Finely dice one of the onions and mix with the tomatoes, spring onion, olive oil and vinegar. Season and place in the fridge. This can be made up to 4 hours ahead of time; just give it a good mix before serving.

2. Thinly slice the other onion and sauté in 1 tbsp vegetable oil until beginning to caramelize. Add the curry paste and fry for another minute, stirring well to prevent it sticking to the pan.

3. Add the coconut milk, bring to a gentle boil and cook for 5 minutes. Taste for seasoning, adding fish sauce, or soy sauce or salt, to taste.

4. Add the carrots and courgette and cook for another 2 minutes, then add the asparagus. Bring back to the boil and take off the heat.

5. Brush the fish with the remaining oil. Heat a pan to medium-high, then place the fish in, skin-side facing down, and cook for 2–3 minutes. Carefully flip over and cook until the flesh is almost cooked through – timing will depend on the thickness of the fillets.

6. To serve, divide the curry among four bowls. Sit a portion of fish on top, then mix the salsa together and spoon on.

For this recipe, it's generally better to buy whole olives and pit them yourself rather than buy commercially pitted ones which aren't always as good. This goes well with soft polenta, chunks of herb-roasted root vegetables, or couscous with lots of fresh herbs mixed in.

LAMB, CHICKPEA AND MUSHROOM STEW WITH MINTED OLIVE SALSA

FOR 4-6 MAIN COURSES

1 red onion, peeled and thinly sliced

6 cloves garlic, peeled and chopped

1 tbsp fresh rosemary leaves or thyme

30 g butter or 2 tbsp olive oil

800 g lamb neck fillet, trimmed of any excessive sinew, cut into 2 cm thick pieces

4 tbsp soy sauce

2 carrots, peeled and thinly sliced

1 x 450 g tin chickpeas, drained and rinsed well

6 field or portobello mushrooms, thickly sliced

1 tbsp flour

5 tbsp cold water

100 g pitted olives

1 small handful mint leaves, shredded

1 small handful flat parsley leaves, shredded

2 tbsp extra virgin olive oil

½ tsp finely grated lemon or orange zest

1. Sauté the onion, garlic and rosemary or thyme in the butter or olive oil until softened; you don't need to caramelize the onion. Add the lamb and cook, stirring constantly, until sealed.

2. Pour on enough water to cover by 2 cm and bring to the boil, then reduce to a simmer and cook for 10 minutes, skimming off any foam that rises to the top.

3. Add the soy sauce, carrots, chickpeas and mushrooms and simmer with the lid on for 45 minutes.

4. Mix the flour with cold water into a smooth paste. Take 150 ml of the stew juices from the pot and mix with the paste. Tip the paste back into the stew and stir it in, then keep cooking for another 20–30 minutes, at which point the lamb will be firm but tender.

5. Roughly chop the olives, then mix with the mint, parsley, extra virgin olive oil and citrus zest.

6. To serve, give the stew a good stir and taste for seasoning. Ladle into bowls and spoon on the salsa.

Very easy to make, this dish is sweet, succulent and juicy – you just need to be good at wrapping presents. I like to serve it in a large bowl, along with shredded coriander mixed with sliced spring onions and chopped chillies to scatter over the top, and let people help themselves.

FIVE-SPICE STEAMED PORK WITH NOODLES AND BROCCOLI FOR 6 MAIN COURSES

3 tbsp demerara sugar

1 tbsp flaky or coarse salt (a little less if using fine salt)

2 tbsp five-spice

1 tsp chilli flakes (more or less to taste)

2 kg boneless pork loin or thick part of the belly, skin scored

500 g dried Chinese egg noodles (or any other noodle)

500 g broccoli, broccolini or sprouting broccoli

1. Preheat oven to 180°C.

2. Lay about 60 cm of foil on your bench and sit a slightly smaller piece of baking paper on top. You're going to wrap the pork up like a parcel and steam it in this.

3. Mix the sugar, salt, five-spice and chilli together and sprinkle one-quarter of it on the paper.

4. Sit the pork on top, skin-side facing up, and sprinkle the rest over. Rub it in thoroughly, then fold the paper over the pork as you would a gift. Wrap this up tightly in the foil until well sealed.

5. Put in a roasting dish and cook for 1½ hours. Take the roasting dish from the oven. Increase the temperature to 200°C.

6. Open up the foil and paper, using scissors if it helps, and baste the pork with the cooking juices. Roast for another 20–30 minutes until the skin begins to bubble – it won't become crispy, though.

7. Cook the noodles and broccoli.

8. To serve, divide the noodles and broccoli among your plates. Cut the pork into chunks and sit it on top, then drizzle with the roasting juices.

I love this way of brining and then cooking the pork belly, as you get a very succulent plump roast with crispy skin. The filling is just as gorgeous, but you can really create any stuffing you'd like, even a traditional bread-type stuffing. Serve with potato salad and green leaves in summer or mash, gravy and steamed greens in colder months.

PEANUT-STUFFED ROLLED PORK BELLY **FOR 8–10 MAIN COURSES**

30 g fine salt

2 kg boneless pork belly, skin scored every 1 cm

1 stem lemongrass

100 g peanuts, toasted and roughly chopped

250 g crunchy peanut butter

½ tsp chilli flakes (more or less to taste)

4 cloves garlic, peeled and finely chopped or grated

3 tbsp fresh tarragon or dill, coarsely chopped

olive oil

flaky salt

1. A day or two before you're planning to eat the pork, you need to brine the belly in a non-reactive, deep-sided roasting dish. Rub the salt into the meat on both sides and leave for 30 minutes. Turn the belly so the skin is facing down, then cover in enough cold water to submerge it. Cover tightly and place in the fridge for 24–48 hours.

2. Preheat the oven to 180°C. Sit a rack in the centre of the oven.

3. Drain the brine from the belly and pat it dry all over. Lay skin-side down on bench.

4. Peel and discard the outer four layers and upper and lower parts of the lemongrass stem, then finely chop the rest. Mix the peanuts, peanut butter, chilli, garlic, herbs and lemongrass together and spread this over the flesh-side of the belly.

5. Roll up tightly and tie with string. Keep it as tight as you can.

6. Line a roasting dish with baking paper (it'll make it easier to clean). Place a cake rack in the dish then sit the belly on, seam facing down.

7. Rub the skin with a little olive oil and sprinkle with flaky salt. Roast for 1¾ hours; the skin should be lovely and golden. Turn the heat up to 240°C and cook for another 15–20 minutes until the crackling has crackled. If it doesn't crackle, turn the grill on medium-high and cook until it does, keeping your eye on it to prevent burning.

8. Leave the belly to rest in a warm place, uncovered, for 15 minutes before removing the string and slicing the meat.

It was the Italians who created this dish originally, and whilst my spicing is a bit off the mark to be authentic, the dish is still absolutely delicious. It's a rich dish, especially with the milky polenta, so just serve with steamed greens or a rocket salad. Use instant polenta grains to make this.

MILK-BAKED PORK WITH PARMESAN POLENTA **FOR 6-8 MAIN COURSES**

2 kg boneless pork loin, skin scored every 1 cm
2 tsp flaky salt
2 litres low-fat milk
6 bay leaves
6 star anise (or 1 tbsp fennel seeds)
1 generous handful thyme on the stalk
2 stalks rosemary, snapped in half
1 small handful sage leaves
1 cinnamon quill, snapped into 4
2 tsp coarsely ground black pepper
250 g instant polenta, sifted
60 g Parmesan, grated

1. Preheat oven to 170°C. Line a large deep-sided roasting dish with baking paper and sit the loin on top, skin-side up. The dish needs to comfortably hold the meat (but not be too large) so it can swim in the milk. Sprinkle with the flaky salt.

2. Place the milk and the next 7 ingredients in a saucepan and bring almost to a simmer. Pour this over the pork, then lay a sheet of baking paper on top of the pork (to cover the skin). Seal the dish really tightly with foil or a tight-fitting lid and bake in the lower part of the oven for 2 hours. Take the lid, foil and paper off and continue to bake for another 45 minutes.

3. Remove the dish from the oven, then carefully remove the pork from the milk and sit in a clean roasting dish. Strain milk through a sieve into a jug and pour 1 litre into a pot. Pour remaining milk back in with the pork and place in the oven, now turned off, to keep warm.

4. Bring the milk to a simmer, then slowly mix in the polenta using a whisk or spoon, avoiding lumps. Cook over a medium-low heat, stirring constantly, until it resembles porridge. It will bubble up like a mud pool if cooked over too high a heat, so make sure you don't burn yourself. Keep cooking for another minute, stirring constantly, then turn off the heat and put a lid on to keep it warm.

5. After 5 minutes the polenta will have swollen up even more. Give it one last stir, stir in the Parmesan, taste for seasoning and you're ready to plate up.

6. To serve, take the pork from the dish and carve as you would a regular roast. Serve on warmed plates with the polenta.

The trick with saffron is that it's better to use a little less than too much – it can have quite an overbearing character. Monkfish on the bone is great in this dish, as are thick flaky fillets like cod or hapuku (in New Zealand).

SAFFRON CLAMS WITH PAN-ROASTED FISH **FOR 4 MAIN COURSES**

400 g clams or cockles, or even mussels, washed to remove grit

250 ml water

100 g shallots, peeled and thinly sliced (2–3 banana shallots or 6 regular shallots)

2 tbsp olive oil

1 tbsp fresh thyme

2 pinches saffron

1 potato, peeled and diced

1 medium carrot, peeled and thinly sliced

10 cm leek, rinsed and thinly sliced into rings

1 thumb ginger, peeled and grated

1 tbsp tarragon leaves

4 x 150 g fish fillets, scales and bones removed

salt and freshly ground black pepper

20 g butter

1. Cook the clams, cockles or mussels first. Place in a wide pot with the water and sit a tight-fitting lid on. Place over high heat and cook for 5 minutes, shaking the pot from side to side every now and then to encourage them to open. After 3 minutes, remove any that have opened and place in a colander over a bowl. After 5 minutes discard any that aren't open. Strain the cooking liquor through a fine sieve. (Occasionally, this liquor and some of the clams can taste a bit muddy from their natural habitat, in which case discard.)

2. Sauté the shallots in half the olive oil until softened then add the thyme, saffron and potato and cook for another minute, stirring all the time. Add the carrot and leek along with 300 ml clam juice or water and bring to a gentle boil.

3. Cook with a lid on until the potato is done. Stir in the ginger and tarragon, turn the heat off and leave the lid on while you cook the fish.

4. Brush the fish with the remaining olive oil and lightly season it. Heat a pan to moderate, add the butter and sit the fish in, skin-side down. Fry for 90 seconds. Carefully flip it over, place a lid on the pan and cook until fish is opaque. A 2 cm thick fillet of salmon or halibut will take around 4 minutes; a fillet of snapper may take less than a minute once flipped over.

5. Once the fish is almost ready, bring the saffron potatoes back to a rapid simmer, add the clams in their shells and warm them through.

6. To serve, place the fish in a bowl and ladle on the clams and saffron broth.

The soft texture of beef fillet contrasts nicely with the crispy crumbs, but they will also work with sirloin or rump steak. I like to serve the dish with mashed potato, a crisp green salad and a grunty meat stock. If you can't get wasabi paste, replace it with horseradish or mustard.

GRILLED BEEF FILLET WITH WASABI CRUMBS FOR 4 MAIN COURSES

600–700 g beef fillet, trimmed of sinew and excess fat

olive oil

50 g butter

1 clove garlic, peeled and finely chopped

1 tbsp wasabi paste (more or less to taste)

50 g coarse breadcrumbs or panko crumbs

1 tbsp chopped chives

salt

meat stock, to serve

1. Turn the oven grill to medium-high.

2. Cut the beef into eight slices and lightly season them, then brush with olive oil.

3. Pan-fry or grill the beef to colour on both sides, then lay on a lightly greased baking tray.

4. Melt the butter and mix with the remaining ingredients and a little salt. Gently but firmly press the mixture on top of each piece of steak.

5. Grill until the crumbs are golden brown and sizzling.

6. Serve on hot plates drizzled with meat stock, if desired.

*This dish combines comfort-food mash with a light, interesting salad, both of which
complement the lamb really well. Lamb rack is very tender, but you can of course make
this from any cut of lamb – simply adjust the cooking times.*

ROAST LAMB RACK WITH FENNEL OLIVE SALAD AND SWEET POTATO MASH **FOR 4 MAIN COURSES**

4 x 4-bone, trimmed lamb racks (about
  200 g per person)
salt and freshly ground black pepper
800 g sweet potato, peeled, ends cut off
  and cut in quarters lengthways
4 tbsp extra virgin olive oil
1 head fennel, trimmed
1 large handful olives, pitted and
  roughly chopped
2 tsp lemon juice
2 tbsp grain mustard
1 small handful mint leaves
1 large handful watercress (don't use
  the stalks if too woody)

1. Preheat oven to 180°C. You can cook the lamb in a large ovenproof pan or seal in a
frying pan and transfer to a roasting dish to finish.

2. Score the fat on the lamb in a crosshatch pattern (it helps it to crisp up) and lightly
season. Heat a pan to moderately hot. Sit the lamb in, fat facing down, and cook for
5–6 minutes until the fat is golden brown. You shouldn't need to add oil to the pan.

3. Place in the oven and cook until done to your liking. Lamb racks are lovely eaten
pink (medium-rare), so cook a rack weighing 200 g for around 12 minutes. Take from
the oven and turn them over so that the fat side is now facing up. Rest in a warm
place while you finish the dish.

4. While the lamb is roasting, put the sweet potato in a pot of hot water with a little
salt and boil until cooked. Drain in a colander, then mash with 2 tbsp olive oil. Taste
for seasoning and keep warm.

5. Slice the fennel thinly into rings, avoiding the stalk end, and place in a bowl with
the olives, lemon juice, mustard, mint and the remaining olive oil. Stir to mix.

6. To serve, divide the mash between four plates, lay some watercress over it and
then sit a lamb rack on top. Spoon on the fennel salad.

I love this pie for its richness, textures and the oyster flavour – please feel free to add more. Because it's quite rich, all you need serve with it is a crunchy green salad dressed with lemon juice and olive oil.

CREAMY POTATO, LEEK, PARMESAN AND OYSTER PIE **FOR 6 MAIN COURSES**

100 g butter
200 g puff pastry
750 g leeks (3–4 leeks), rinsed and sliced
4 cloves garlic, peeled and sliced
2 tbsp fresh thyme or oregano
4 tbsp flour
400 ml cream
1 tsp chilli sauce (more or less to taste)
salt and freshly ground black pepper
5 large potatoes, peeled and sliced
  5 mm thick
100 g Parmesan or Cheddar, grated
18 oysters (or as many more as you like)
1 large handful parsley, roughly
  chopped
1 egg, beaten, for egg-wash

1. Preheat oven to 190°C. Generously butter the bottom of a 1.5 litre pie dish (24–30 cm in diameter). Roll the pastry out into a circle 2 cm wider than the inside rim of the pie dish. Put to one side in a cool spot.

2. Place the remaining butter in a pan and cook over a moderate heat until it begins to sizzle. Add the leeks, garlic and herbs and sauté until collapsed, stirring frequently; around 15 minutes.

3. Sprinkle on the flour and stir it in, then add the cream, chilli sauce, salt and pepper and bring just to the boil, stirring constantly. Take off the heat.

4. While the leeks are cooking, bring a pot of salted water to the boil. Add the sliced potatoes, dropping them in a few at a time to keep them separated so they cook evenly, then gently boil until almost cooked. Carefully tip into a colander and leave for a few minutes. Stir gently into the leek mixture along with the cheese, oysters and parsley and taste for seasoning.

5. Spoon the filling into the pie dish and flatten the top with the back of a spoon. Brush the egg-wash around the inside lip of the dish and press the pastry onto the filling, making sure there are no air bubbles. Press the edge of the pastry against the rim of the dish to seal it, then trim off any excess. Prick the top of the pie with a fork a dozen times and brush with the remaining egg-wash.

6. Sit the pie dish on a baking tray in the centre of the oven and bake until the pastry is golden brown; about 25–35 minutes.

A deliciously simple stew, this is great served with buttery mashed potatoes, steamed rice or egg noodles. You can also stir in lots of finely chopped raw ginger as you serve it for a really refreshing taste.

CHILLIED BEEF AND CASHEW STEW WITH CORIANDER SALSA **FOR 6 MAIN COURSES**

1 kg diced stewing beef, trimmed of excess gristle

1 tsp smoked paprika (either sweet or spicy/piquant)

1 red chilli, sliced (more or less to taste)

salt

2 tbsp vegetable oil

300 g baby onions, peeled

12 cloves garlic, separated but unpeeled

200 g baby carrots, skins scrubbed and stalks removed

2 x 400 g tins peeled chopped tomatoes

6 sprigs thyme

50 ml soy sauce

hot water

100 g cashews, toasted

3 spring onions, thinly sliced

1 large handful coriander, shredded

2 tbsp lime juice

1 tsp finely grated lime zest

2 tbsp extra virgin olive oil

1. Mix the beef with the smoked paprika, chilli and a little salt and put to one side.

2. Heat the oil in a heavy-based pan and add the onions, garlic and carrots. Cook over moderate heat to evenly colour the vegetables, stirring often.

3. Once done, remove with a slotted spoon but keep the oil in the pan.

4. Add the beef to the pan and brown the meat all over.

5. Add the tomatoes, thyme and soy sauce, along with the cooked onions, garlic and carrots. Add enough hot water to cover the meat.

6. Bring to a boil, then reduce heat to a simmer. Put a lid on and cook either on the stove top or in the oven at 150°C for 2½ hours, stirring the stew several times while it's cooking. If the cooking liquid begins to dry out, top it up with boiling water.

7. After 1 hour's cooking, stir in the cashews.

8. Mix the spring onions, coriander, lime juice and zest and olive oil together.

9. To serve, ladle the stew into bowls and spoon on the salsa.

This barley 'stew' is much like a risotto and is a really delicious base on which to serve the salmon. The addition of smoked salmon in the stew, along with the salmon caviar, makes this triply delicious.

PAN-FRIED SALMON ON CREAMY SMOKED SALMON AND BROAD BEAN BARLEY FOR 4 MAIN COURSES

4 x 160 g pieces salmon fillet, skin and
  bones removed
salt and freshly ground black pepper
light olive oil or sunflower oil
100 g pearl barley
4 sprigs fresh sage
700 ml water
2 spring onions, cut into 1 cm lengths
60 g butter
200 ml cream
2 strips lemon peel (use a potato peeler)
200 g broad beans, boiled for 2 minutes
  then drained and podded (frozen or
  fresh)
60 g smoked salmon, either flaked hot-
  smoked or thinly sliced cold-smoked
  (optional)
2 tbsp salmon caviar (optional)

1. Lightly season the salmon and leave to come to room temperature. Brush with a little oil.

2. Rinse the barley briefly in a sieve under cold water, then place in a pan with the sage stalks (not the leaves just yet) and water. Bring to the boil, then rapidly simmer for 20 minutes until al dente. Add 1 tsp salt, turn the heat off and leave to sit for 5 minutes before draining.

3. Sauté the spring onions in half the butter until the butter begins to colour and the spring onions soften. Add the cream and lemon peel and bring to the boil. Add the barley and simmer for 10 minutes. Stir in the broad beans and smoked salmon (if using).

4. Fry or grill the salmon on both sides until it's rare – nice and pink in the centre. Cooking time will depend on the thickness of the fillets.

5. While the salmon is cooking, heat up another small pot with the remaining butter and the sage leaves. Cook over medium-high heat until the leaves crisp up and the butter turns golden. Take from the heat but keep warm.

6. To serve, divide the barley among four warm plates and sit a piece of salmon on top. Drizzle with the sage and its butter, and spoon over the salmon caviar (if using) last of all.

Scallops are a richly textured shellfish, which lack the briny taste of the oyster and the robustness of the mussel. Small Queen scallops don't need a lot of cooking, just 90 seconds in total, but large diver-caught ones will need about 3–4 minutes. Scallops become tough if overcooked, so be careful. This purée is also fantastic with grilled fish, roast leg of lamb or poached chicken.

SAUTÉED SCALLOPS ON JERUSALEM ARTICHOKE AND TRUFFLE-OIL PURÉE

FOR 4 STARTERS

250 g peeled Jerusalem artichokes (plus
   1 unpeeled artichoke to make the
   crisps)
200 ml cream
ice-cold water
vegetable oil
salt and freshly ground black pepper
1 tsp lemon juice
1 tsp white truffle oil or lemon-infused
   olive oil
500 g trimmed scallops
2 tbsp micro-cress or snipped chives

1. Cut the peeled artichokes in half lengthways. Place in a pan with the cream, adding hot water if they're not covered. Bring to the boil, turn to a simmer and place a lid on. After 15 minutes, take the lid off and cook until the cream has reduced by half and the artichokes are tender, just like a cooked potato.

2. While they're cooking, make the crisps from the unpeeled artichoke. Scrub the skin really well. Slice as thin as possible (a mandolin or potato peeler is ideal), then rinse in ice-cold water and gently pat dry.

3. Heat 4 cm of vegetable oil to 160°C and cook the crisps in several batches until golden, gently stirring and turning them often to cook evenly. Remove with a slotted spoon and drain on kitchen paper. Sprinkle with salt while hot.

4. Drain the boiled artichokes in a colander or sieve sitting over a bowl. Purée until smooth, adding enough of the cream they were cooked in as needed. It should have some body to it, so don't thin it out too much. Mix in the lemon juice and oil and season with salt and pepper. Keep covered and warm while you cook the scallops.

5. Brush the scallops with vegetable oil and lightly season. Heat up a heavy-based frying pan or grill-pan until hot. Place the scallops in quickly (to ensure they all cook the same amount of time) and cook until golden. Turn them over and cook until golden on the other side and medium-rare.

6. To serve, spoon the purée onto warm plates. Sit the scallops on top, garnish with the crisps and sprinkle with the cress or chives.

Duck legs come in varying sizes. For a main course, you're after legs weighing around 150 g each, otherwise serve two per portion.

VANILLA-BRAISED DUCK LEG ON GINGER COCONUT RICE WITH MANGO SALSA **FOR 4 MAIN COURSES**

4–8 duck legs (depending on size)
2 spring onions, cut into 4 pieces
½ vanilla bean, split in half lengthways
½ tsp coarsely ground black pepper
1 small handful thyme leaves and stalks
2 cloves garlic, crushed
4 tbsp soy sauce
400 ml hot water
200 g basmati rice
1 tsp finely chopped ginger
250 ml coconut milk
¼ tsp fine salt
180 ml cold water
1 smallish red onion, peeled and thinly
  sliced
1 tsp coarse salt
½ mango, peeled, flesh taken from the
  stone, diced
a few parsley leaves, torn
1 small bunch coriander, cut through
  the stalk into 2 cm lengths

1. Preheat oven to 180°C.

2. Choose a deep-sided roasting dish that will be just large enough to hold the duck legs in one layer. Put the spring onions, vanilla bean, black pepper, thyme and garlic in the bottom and sit the legs on top, skin-side facing up.

3. Mix the soy into the hot water and pour this over the legs.

4. Lay a sheet of baking paper loosely on top of the legs and seal the dish tightly with foil. Bake for 2 hours. Remove the foil and baking paper from the roasting dish and continue to cook until the skin is golden brown.

5. Rinse the rice in a sieve under running water, then place in a medium pot with the ginger, coconut milk and fine salt. Add cold water and put onto high heat. Bring to the boil, then put a lid on and simmer for 12 minutes. Turn the heat off, but keep the lid on and leave to rest for 10 minutes before stirring with a fork.

6. While that's cooking, make the salsa. Place the sliced onion in a bowl with the coarse salt and rub together quite firmly for 10 seconds. Leave for a few minutes, then rinse under cold water and drain. Mix with the mango, parsley and coriander.

7. To serve, divide the rice among four plates, sit a duck leg on each and spoon on the cooking juices. Give the salsa a mix and spoon it on top.

This hearty and spicy stew takes its inspiration from South-East Asia. It's rich and comforting and just needs to be served with steamed rice, noodles or boiled potatoes.

SPICY PORK STEW WITH COCONUT AND PEAS **FOR 8 MAIN COURSES**

3 onions, peeled and sliced

2 red chillies, stalks removed, cut into 4 pieces (more or less to taste)

2 thumbs ginger, peeled and sliced

2 tbsp coriander seeds

1 tbsp fennel seeds

1 tbsp turmeric

50 ml cider vinegar or white vinegar

1 x 400 ml tin coconut milk

2 tbsp vegetable oil

10 cloves garlic, peeled and halved

1 tbsp cumin seeds

1.5 kg pork shoulder, cut into large dice

50 g desiccated coconut

1 tsp fine salt

100 ml water

salt and freshly ground black pepper

300 g frozen peas

1. Place half the onions in a blender with the chillies, ginger, coriander and fennel seeds, turmeric, vinegar and coconut milk. Purée to a coarse paste.

2. Heat up a large pot and add the oil, the remaining onions, the garlic and cumin seeds and fry until the onions are caramelized, stirring often.

3. Add the pork and desiccated coconut and continue to cook for 3 minutes, stirring constantly.

4. Add the chilli purée along with the fine salt and water.

5. Cover the mixture with a sheet of baking paper cut to the same diameter as the pot (a cartouche) and bring to the boil. Place on a tight-fitting lid and either continue to cook over a low heat on the stove or place in an oven at 170°C for 2 hours.

6. Adjust seasoning, give it a good stir, and cook for another 20 minutes.

7. Stir in the peas a few minutes before serving.

This is meltingly delicious – the long, slow cooking renders the tasty meat tender and succulent. Mum cooks hers in a large crock pot-type cooker but you can also do it in the oven in a tightly sealed roasting dish. Mutton is older than lamb and therefore more developed in taste, which I really like when cooked like this. If you can't find boned shoulder then cook it on the bone; it will weigh 1.5–2kg. Serve with mashed spuds, minted peas and gravy made from the pan juices.

MUM'S SLOW-BAKED MUTTON SHOULDER **FOR 4-6 MAIN COURSES**

1 mutton shoulder, boned and rolled (about 1.2 kg)

sea salt and freshly ground black pepper

1 head garlic, cloves separated but not peeled

1 onion, peeled and quartered

1 carrot, peeled and cut into 4

3 sprigs rosemary or several more of thyme

2 bay leaves

150 ml hot water (or 300 ml for second method)

1. Season the mutton all over with plenty of sea salt and black pepper.

2. Place all the vegetables and herbs in the bottom of a large slow cooker and sit the mutton on top. Pour on 150 ml hot water, then set the cooker to 120°C and cook for 6 hours.

3. Alternatively, preheat oven to 160°C. Place the vegetables and herbs in the bottom of a deep-sided roasting dish, sit the shoulder on top and add 300 ml hot water. Cover first with baking paper and then seal tightly with foil or a lid. Bake for 4 hours.

This stew is lovely, earthy and rich, and it becomes more characterful the more meats you use; even wild duck and poultry work well. You can cook it in a crock pot, on top of the stove or in the oven at 170°C. Serve with buttered cabbage or broccoli and a big bowl of mash or a vegetable gratin.

MIXED MEAT AND ALE STEW **FOR 8 MAIN COURSES**

olive oil

1.5 kg diced boneless meat (I use a
   mixture of beef topside, pork belly,
   mutton leg and venison shoulder)

2 onions, peeled and thickly sliced

12 cloves garlic, peeled and sliced

4 bay leaves

2 tbsp fresh rosemary leaves

1 tbsp sweet smoked paprika or regular
   paprika

500 ml ale

1 litre meat stock

4 tbsp soy sauce

2 cinnamon quills, snapped in half

10 pitted prunes, halved

1 eggplant, stem removed, diced

300 g baby beetroot or baby carrots,
   skins scrubbed

salt and freshly ground black pepper

100 ml crème fraîche

1. Heat up a large pot with a little oil and brown the meat. It will be easier to do it in several batches.

2. Once the meat is done, caramelize the onions and garlic in a little more oil.

3. Add the bay leaves, rosemary and paprika and cook for another few minutes, stirring often.

4. Return the meat to the pot along with the ale, stock, soy sauce, cinnamon and prunes and bring to the boil, stirring as it heats up.

5. Place on a tight-fitting lid and either continue to cook over a low heat on the stove or place in an oven at 170°C for 1½ hours.

6. Stir in the eggplant and beetroot or carrots and continue cooking for another hour.

7. To serve, taste for seasoning, then stir in the crème fraîche.

This dish can be cooked in a casserole dish or in one of the many brilliant slow-cookers for sale these days (we used to call them crock pots in the '70s). Serve simply with boiled white rice or mashed potatoes and steamed greens.

BRAISED PORK BELLY WITH ORANGE **FOR 4-6 MAIN COURSES**

1 kg boneless pork belly, cut into large dice
oil, for cooking
300 g shallots, peeled but kept whole
8 cloves garlic, peeled and sliced
8 cardamom pods or 6 star anise (or a mixture of both), crushed
2 bay leaves
2 small oranges
350 ml vegetable or chicken stock
150 ml dry sherry (or extra stock)
80 ml soy sauce

1. Preheat oven to 170°C.

2. Fry the pork in a heavy-based pan or casserole dish with a little oil to colour evenly, stirring as it cooks to prevent it sticking.

3. Remove the meat with a slotted spoon, keeping the fats in the pan.

4. Add the shallots, garlic, spices and bay leaves to the same pan and sauté until coloured.

5. Cut the top and bottom off the oranges and slice the body 5 mm thick without peeling. Add to the pan and fry to soften.

6. Add the stock, sherry and soy sauce and bring to the boil.

7. Return the pork to the pan and stir it in, cover with a tight-fitting lid, then place in the oven and cook for 2 hours. Alternatively, you can cook it on top of the stove at a gentle simmer.

8. Give it a good stir every 30 minutes, then when it's ready taste for seasoning.

CHAPTER SIX

SIDES AND CONDIMENTS

This Catalan dish is similar to French ratatouille and, like ratatouille, it tastes even better the day after you make it. It's fabulous served as a dish in its own right with crusty bread and green salad, or alongside grilled pork, lamb or fish, or on bruschetta with mozzarella or goat's cheese.

ESCALIVADA FOR 6-8 AS A SIDE DISH

3 red capsicums
2 large tomatoes
1 eggplant
2 red onions, peeled and cut into ½ cm thick rings (discard the top and bottom)
6 spring onions, only use the bottom half
4 cloves garlic, peeled and finely grated
½ tsp finely grated lemon zest
2 tbsp lemon juice
4 tbsp extra virgin olive oil
1 handful mint and basil leaves, torn

1. Grill the capsicums and tomatoes (don't oil them) on a barbecue, over a gas flame or in the oven until their skins blister and blacken and they begin to soften. Place in a plastic bag.

2. Cook the eggplant the same way, but prick it several times before doing so. You need to grill it until the skin blackens and you can almost squeeze it inwards. Place this in a separate plastic bag.

3. Grill the onions (or cook in a skillet) on both sides until marked and a little softened. Place on a plate to cool.

4. Grill the spring onions all over until softened and slightly blackened, then peel off any badly burnt pieces while still warm.

5. Mix the garlic with the lemon zest and juice in a large bowl.

6. Once the vegetables have cooled enough for you to handle, take from their bags, peel their skins and remove stalks. Cut the capsicums in half and remove the seeds.

7. Split the eggplant in half lengthways and gently squeeze out excess moisture, as this can be a little bitter. Cut into thin strips and add to the lemon in the bowl. Cut the capsicums and tomatoes into strips and add to the bowl.

8. Slice the red onions and spring onions, add to the other vegetables with the olive oil and herbs, and mix well. Season to taste.

This salad accompanies steamed fish, roast chicken or grilled lamb chops really well. It's delicious topped with crumbled feta or goat's cheese and is also good in a burger.

MINTED CUCUMBER SALAD WITH PISTACHIO DRESSING FOR 4 AS A SIDE DISH

1 large cucumber
1 tsp salt
1 tsp runny honey
3 tbsp lemon juice
1 large handful mint leaves, shred the
    large ones but keep the smaller ones
    whole
50 g shelled pistachio nuts
2 tbsp olive oil
freshly ground pepper

1. Peel and slice the cucumber really thinly and toss with the salt in a bowl, then leave for 20 minutes.

2. Place the cucumber in a colander, gently rinse with cold water and leave to drain for 10 minutes.

3. Dissolve the honey in half the lemon juice and toss with the cucumber in a bowl.

4. Mix in the mint, cover the bowl and leave in the fridge to chill for a few hours.

5. Roughly chop the pistachios and place in a small pan with the oil. Cook over a moderate heat until the oil begins to sizzle a little and the nuts colour slightly – don't cook them for too long, though, so they keep their lovely colour.

6. Tip the hot nuts and oil over the cucumber, along with the remaining lemon juice. Add a few grinds of pepper, mix everything together and taste for seasoning.

This is a terrific side dish to accompany a main course, as it goes really well with roast or poached meats and oily fish like mackerel, tuna and salmon. It can be eaten hot or cold and you can add lots of picked herbs like chervil, mint or basil, depending on what you're going to serve it with.

ROAST CAULIFLOWER AND OLIVES
FOR 4-6 AS A SIDE DISH

1 medium cauliflower
2 handfuls mixed olives
1 small handful sage leaves
salt and freshly ground black pepper
4 tbsp olive oil
1 juicy lemon

1. Preheat oven to 220°C.

2. Remove the outer leaves from the cauliflower and cut the florets from the stem. Cut any large florets in half lengthways. Place in a roasting dish with the olives and sage.

3. Season with pepper and a little salt (the olives may be salty already) and drizzle over the oil. Toss it all together.

4. Roast in the top half of the oven until the cauliflower begins to colour, stirring from time to time, about 20 minutes.

5. Take from the oven, squeeze on the lemon juice, and it's ready.

Much like a coleslaw, this salad is great served with grilled meats, especially pork chops or sausages. Kohlrabi is an interesting vegetable, as it is delicious served either raw or cooked. However, if you can't find it, use 200 g peeled celeriac or nashi pear instead.

KOHLRABI, SAVOY CABBAGE, WALNUT, GRAPEFRUIT AND PEAR SALAD **FOR 6-8 AS A SIDE DISH**

1 large kohlrabi
¼ firm Savoy cabbage
2 ripe pears
1 large grapefruit
125 ml plain yoghurt, sour cream or
  mayonnaise
2 tbsp roughly chopped dill
salt and freshly ground black pepper
2 tbsp extra virgin olive oil
100 g walnuts, roughly chopped

1. Peel the kohlrabi, julienne it and place in a large bowl.

2. Cut the core from the cabbage, then shred it as thinly as you can and put in the bowl.

3. Cut the pears into quarters, remove the core, then thinly slice and add to the bowl.

4. Cut the skin and pith from the grapefruit with a sharp knife, then cut the segments out. Add to the bowl and squeeze any juice from the membranes into the bowl.

5. Add the yoghurt, sour cream or mayonnaise and dill and mix in with a little salt and pepper.

6. Place the oil in a small pan over medium-low heat and add the walnuts. Cook until golden, shaking the pan from time to time.

7. Pour the oil and walnuts over the salad and mix everything together. Serve within a few hours.

This is a creamy purée, yet it is dairy-free which suits a lot of people. You can buy silken tofu from health food stores and Japanese supermarkets. It often comes pre-packaged and is much smoother than regular tofu, but the latter will also work.

PUMPKIN, TOFU AND GINGER PURÉE **FOR 6–8 AS A SIDE DISH**

1 onion, peeled and thinly sliced

1 tbsp vegetable oil

1 thumb ginger, peeled and thinly sliced (or use candied or sushi ginger)

¼ tsp turmeric (or a few saffron strands)

500 g peeled pumpkin, thinly sliced

2 tbsp lemon juice

4 tbsp water

400 g silken tofu

1 tbsp toasted sesame oil

salt and freshly ground black pepper

1. Sauté the onion in the vegetable oil until just beginning to caramelize, stirring frequently. Stir in the ginger and turmeric (or saffron) and cook for another 3 minutes.

2. Add the pumpkin, lemon juice and water. Put a lid on and cook over moderate heat until the pumpkin is cooked through. Stir from time to time to prevent the vegetables burning on the bottom.

3. Slice the tofu into 8 pieces and lay on absorbent kitchen paper.

4. Once the pumpkin is ready, take the lid off the pan and continue cooking until most of the liquid has evaporated.

5. Put the pumpkin in a food processor with the tofu and sesame oil and purée to a fine texture.

6. Taste for seasoning and serve hot.

Having a few different pestos at hand is a good thing, as they're incredibly versatile.
How thick or thin they need be is really up to how you'll serve them. A slightly runny
one is great drizzled over grilled meat or fish, and a thicker one is good tossed through
pasta or mashed into potatoes.

PESTO

GINGER WALNUT PESTO MAKES 300 g

100 g walnuts, toasted
60 g crystallized or candied stem ginger
   (or 2 tsp grated fresh ginger)
1 small handful parsley leaves
60 g Parmesan, grated
150 ml olive oil
salt and freshly ground black pepper

1. Place the walnuts, ginger and parsley in a food processor and pulse to coarse crumbs.

2. Add the Parmesan and pulse again briefly, then add the oil and pulse to a chunky paste.

3. Taste for seasoning.

ROCKET ALMOND PESTO MAKES 270 g

1 large handful rocket, washed and
   patted dry (or watercress for a more
   peppery taste)
1 clove garlic, peeled
60 g almonds, toasted
60 g Parmesan, grated
125 ml olive oil
salt and freshly ground black pepper

1. Roughly chop the rocket. Place in a food processor with the garlic and almonds and pulse to a coarse paste.

2. Add the Parmesan and pulse again briefly, then add the oil and pulse to a smooth paste.

3. Taste for seasoning.

SMOKED PAPRIKA, HAZELNUT AND MINT PESTO MAKES 290 g

125 ml olive oil

2 tsp sweet smoked paprika

100 g hazelnuts, toasted and skins rubbed off

50 g Manchego or Parmesan, finely grated

1 generous handful mint leaves

1 tsp dried mint (optional, but it adds a depth of flavour)

salt and freshly ground black pepper

1. Heat 1 tbsp oil in a small pan with the smoked paprika and cook over low heat for a minute, gently stirring constantly – this toasts the paprika and gives it a deeper taste. Make sure the oil doesn't get too hot, as it could burn.

2. Tip into a food processor with the nuts and pulse to break the nuts up, then leave to cool for a few minutes.

3. Add everything else and pulse to a coarse paste.

4. Taste for seasoning.

This relish goes well with pork and duck, as it's quite tangy and fruity. However, it will spice up a roast chicken or a grilled piece of fish.

COCONUT, PINEAPPLE AND CHILLI RELISH **MAKES 1 LITRE**

1 medium pineapple
4 onions, peeled and sliced
vegetable oil, for frying
2–3 chillies, sliced into rings (more or less to taste)
8 cloves garlic, peeled and sliced
1 tbsp ground allspice
300 g caster sugar
300 ml cider vinegar or white wine vinegar
100 g desiccated coconut, lightly toasted
300 ml unsweetened coconut milk

1. Peel the pineapple, cut into quarters and remove the core. Either blitz in a food processor until coarsely chopped or grate it.

2. In a large pot, sauté the onions in vegetable oil until caramelized.

3. Add the chillies, garlic and allspice and sauté for another minute.

4. Add the pineapple, sugar and vinegar, bring to a boil, then put a lid on and cook over a low heat for 30 minutes. Stir occasionally to prevent it sticking to the bottom.

5. Add the desiccated coconut and the coconut milk. Bring to a boil, then cook uncovered to evaporate most of the liquid.

6. Pour into hot sterilized jars and seal while hot. Once they've cooled, store in the fridge and use after two days but within 2–3 weeks.

The addition of soy and balsamic produces a lovely dark red dish which complements its earthy characteristics. It's lovely served alongside roast red meats and game. Once everything has been added you can cook this in the oven at 120°C if you prefer to take it off the stove.

BRAISED RED CABBAGE WITH PEAR AND STAR ANISE **FOR 12 OR MORE AS A SIDE DISH**

1 red cabbage
2 red onions, peeled and sliced
4 tbsp extra virgin olive oil
4 cloves garlic, peeled and sliced
2 thumbs ginger, peeled and julienned
150 g sultanas, raisins or currants
200 ml balsamic vinegar
500 ml pear or apple juice
2 cinnamon quills
1 small handful star anise
125 ml soy sauce (if you're using
   very salty soy sauce, add less at the
   beginning and adjust towards the end
   of cooking)
freshly ground black pepper

1. Cut the cabbage into quarters, remove the core and shred ½ cm thick.

2. Sauté the onions in the oil until softened.

3. Add the garlic and ginger and cook until the onions caramelize, stirring frequently.

4. Add the sultanas, raisins or currants and cook until they begin to puff up.

5. Stir in the vinegar and cook until it evaporates.

6. Add the juice, cinnamon and star anise and bring to the boil.

7. Add the cabbage and pour on the soy sauce. Put a lid on and bring to the boil.

8. Cook for 5 minutes, then mix it all together and turn to a simmer.

9. Put the lid back on and cook for 1 hour, checking from time to time that it doesn't boil dry. Once the cabbage has become quite tender, taste for seasoning.

The most important thing to remember when cooking bok choy is that it prefers to be cooked briefly over a very high heat in a wok or steamed for a short amount of time. If you don't have a wok, it can be cooked in a wide frying pan so long as you have good heat. This is lovely served with steamed or poached fish and basmati or jasmine rice.

WOK-FRIED BOK CHOY WITH GINGER, PEANUTS AND OYSTER SAUCE **FOR 4-6 AS A SIDE DISH**

600 g bok choy (or pak choy)

3 tbsp peanut oil (sunflower or canola oil also work)

1 tbsp chopped ginger

2 cloves garlic, peeled and chopped

80 g roasted peanuts (chunky peanut butter will do at a stretch)

4 tbsp oyster sauce (use soy sauce if you'd prefer)

1. Cut the base from the bok choy to separate the leaves. If they're large cut them vertically through the stalk, and if they're very small leave them whole.

2. Wash in cold water and drain in a colander. It's important that they retain some moisture, though, so don't spin them in a salad spinner.

3. Heat a wok over high heat then add half of the oil, carefully swish it around the base of the wok and immediately add all of the bok choy (assuming your wok is large enough to take it – if not, cook in several batches).

4. Using a large spoon or tongs, toss the bok choy every 5 seconds or so for 1 minute until it wilts. Tip into a bowl.

5. Place the wok back on the heat and add the remaining oil, ginger, garlic and peanuts. Cook over a high heat, stirring all the time, until the garlic becomes golden.

6. Return the bok choy to the wok along with the oyster sauce and toss it all together, then serve immediately.

Both of these side dishes go really well with any type of lamb in the classic way that mint always does. However, they also team well with roast chicken and grilled or pan-fried oily fish such as tuna, salmon and mackerel.

MINTED PEA SALSA FOR 4 AS A SIDE DISH

200 g peas, frozen or fresh
1 spring onion, thinly sliced
1 handful mint leaves
4 tbsp extra virgin olive oil
2 shallots, peeled and thinly sliced into
  rings
2 tbsp rice vinegar or cider vinegar
salt and freshly ground black pepper

1. Boil the peas in lightly salted water until just cooked, then drain and refresh under cold running water.

2. Place half the peas in a food processor with the sliced spring onion and the mint leaves and pulse to a coarse texture – do not purée. Tip into a bowl and mix with the remaining peas and the olive oil. Leave for 30 minutes.

3. Mix the shallots with the vinegar and leave for 30 minutes as well.

4. Mix the peas with the shallots and season.

5. The vinegar will cause the peas to discolour, so serve within a few hours.

MINTED GARLIC YOGHURT FOR 4 AS A SIDE DISH

300 ml plain thick yoghurt
1 clove garlic, finely chopped
2 tbsp lemon juice
1 tbsp extra virgin olive oil
1 handful mint leaves, shredded
1 tsp flaky salt
50 ml cold water
salt and freshly ground black pepper

1. Mix the yoghurt, garlic and lemon juice together.

2. Mix in everything else and leave for at least 1 hour to settle and mellow.

3. Taste for seasoning, mix again and serve chilled.

Serve as a garnish for roast chicken or other meats at a roast dinner, or on the buffet at your next barbecue.

BRAISED BABY GEMS WITH PEAS AND CHORIZO **FOR 4 AS A SIDE DISH**

1 large onion, peeled and thinly sliced
50 ml olive oil or butter
200 g cooking chorizo, sliced ½ cm thick (or lardons or diced smoked bacon)
4 baby gem lettuces or baby cos, halved and washed
250 g peas, fresh or frozen
250 ml vegetable or light chicken stock
1 handful roughly chopped flat parsley
salt and freshly ground black pepper

1. Sauté the onion over medium heat in the oil or butter until beginning to caramelize.

2. Add the chorizo and continue to cook on a moderate heat until the fat has rendered out and the mixture is looking jammy.

3. Put the baby gems or cos in the pan, cut-side down, and cook for 1 minute, then add the peas and stock.

4. Place a lid on the pan and bring to a boil, give it a good stir and reduce to a simmer. Cook for 5 minutes.

5. Just before serving, stir in the parsley, grind in lots of black pepper and taste for salt.

Café Habana (not Havana) is the coolest Mexican diner-restaurant on the corner of Prince and Elizabeth streets in NoLita, New York City. I have eaten their corn a zillion times and never tire of it. Yum!

CAFÉ HABANA-INSPIRED GRILLED SWEET CORN **FOR 2 AS A BRUNCH SNACK**

olive oil or sunflower oil
2 corn cobs, husks removed
4 tbsp cream cheese
6 tbsp finely grated Parmesan
ground chipotle chilli powder, paprika
   or chilli flakes, to taste
1 lime, cut into wedges

1. You may prefer to cut the corn cobs in half and serve two pieces per portion rather than one large cob – it's up to you. Heat up a skillet, the oven grill or the barbecue.

2. Rub a little olive or sunflower oil over the cobs.

3. Mix the cream cheese with half the Parmesan.

4. Cook the corn until golden all around, turning the cobs as they colour. If cooking in a pan or skillet, it pays to put a lid on the pan to stop the odd kernel popping.

5. Take from the pan and spread with the cream cheese mix.

6. Sprinkle with the reserved Parmesan and ground chilli.

7. Serve with lime wedges, squeezing the juice over as you eat them.

This Turkish-inspired dish is always a favourite of mine in summer. It's important to note that the beans are not meant to be crunchy, and they will lose some of their green colour if not eaten until the following day – which is totally fine. What they lose in colour they gain in flavour.

TURKISH-STYLE BEANS AND TOMATOES WITH DILL AND CHILLI
FOR 6 AS A SIDE DISH

1 onion, peeled and thinly sliced

3 cloves garlic, peeled and sliced

1 red chilli, roughly chopped (more or less to taste)

2 tbsp sunflower oil or canola oil

2 tomatoes, cut into large chunks (unpeeled)

200 g green beans, trimmed

3 tbsp water

½ tsp salt

100 g podded broad beans, grey skin removed if they're large

freshly ground black pepper

2 tbsp extra virgin olive oil

2 tbsp chopped dill (use the stalks and keep it chunky)

1½ tbsp lemon juice

1. In a pot with a tight-fitting lid, sauté the onion, garlic and chilli in the oil until softened, but uncoloured. Stir in the tomatoes and cook for 1 minute, then add the green beans, water and salt.

2. Put the lid on and cook over a high heat for 2 minutes, then turn down to medium and cook for a further 2 minutes.

3. Stir in the broad beans, put the lid back on, and cook for another 2 minutes.

4. Take off the heat and stir in some pepper, the olive oil and the dill. Leave to cool, then stir in the lemon juice.

5. This is best made at least 6 hours before you want to eat it, or even the day before. Eat at room temperature.

These are delicious served with pretty much any meat or fish, or served as part of a vegetable buffet. If you can't get baby carrots, cut larger ones into chunks.

ROAST BABY CARROTS WITH GINGER, GARLIC AND RED ONION
FOR 6-8 AS A SIDE DISH

500 g baby carrots, skins lightly
   scrubbed
1 red onion, peeled and thinly sliced
2 cloves garlic, peeled and thinly sliced
1 fat thumb ginger, peeled and
   julienned
3 tbsp extra virgin olive oil
sea salt and freshly ground black
   pepper
2 tbsp water

1. Preheat oven to 200°C.

2. Line a roasting tray with baking paper and place the carrots, onions, garlic, ginger and oil in. Toss everything together and season with salt and pepper.

3. Drizzle over the water and place another sheet of baking paper loosely on top. Roast for 20 minutes, then take the paper off and give it all a good mix.

4. Roast another 5–10 minutes until cooked, depending on the size of the carrots.

This salad is a gorgeous deep red colour and makes a good side dish to have beside the usual greens, leafy salads and the like. Wear gloves when preparing it or your hands will get badly stained. This can be made with different coloured beetroot, but then it wouldn't be called red salad…

RED SALAD **FOR 6-8 AS A SIDE DISH**

2–3 raw red beetroot
3 tbsp red wine vinegar
2 tsp honey
1 tsp flaky salt
3 red capsicums
2 handfuls cherry tomatoes, halved
2 handfuls cherries, pitted and halved
1 large radicchio, shredded
50 ml extra virgin olive oil
salt and freshly ground black pepper

1. Peel the beetroot, then grate finely and put in a bowl.

2. Mix in the vinegar, honey and flaky salt, then leave for 20 minutes.

3. Grill or roast the capsicums and cool in a plastic bag. Peel the skin from them, discard the stem and seeds, then thinly slice and add to the beetroot.

4. Add the tomatoes, cherries and radicchio to the salad along with the olive oil and lots of freshly ground black pepper.

5. Mix everything and leave for 10 minutes before tossing again. Taste for seasoning.

This side dish is a wonderful accompaniment to a grilled steak or piece of grilled salmon or tuna. Or, eat it as it is with lots of picked coriander, mint and spring onions sprinkled on top. It's best eaten slightly warm or at room temperature. You'll have more chilli-miso mixture than you need, but it keeps in the fridge for 2 weeks and is great added to soups and stews or rubbed over fish fillets before baking.

BAKED CHILLI-MISO EGGPLANT WITH TOFU GINGER DRESSING **FOR 6 AS A SIDE DISH**

1 red onion, peeled and diced

½ red chilli, finely chopped (more or less to taste)

2 tsp sesame seeds

2 tsp sesame oil

3 tbsp miso paste (pale or darker miso pastes will all work well)

150 ml mirin (or 4 tbsp sugar and 100 ml water)

1 thumb ginger, peeled and finely chopped or grated

3 tbsp rice vinegar, cider vinegar or lemon juice

1½ tbsp soy sauce

150 g silken tofu (see note on page 209)

3 eggplants

1. Preheat oven to 180°C. Line a baking tray with baking paper and place the oven rack in the centre of the oven.

2. Sauté the onion, chilli and sesame seeds in the sesame oil until beginning to caramelize.

3. Stir in the miso paste, then add the mirin and bring to the boil.

4. Turn to a simmer and cook for 1 minute, then take off the heat.

5. Purée the ginger, vinegar or lemon juice, soy and tofu until it resembles a creamy mayonnaise. You can do this with a stick blender or use a small food processor or blender.

6. Cut the stem off the eggplants and cut them in half lengthways. Score the cut side in a crisscross fashion, avoiding cutting through to the skin.

7. Spread a tablespoon of the miso mixture on each cut side and rub it into the scored flesh. Lay the eggplants on the baking tray and cook for 15–20 minutes, just to the point where the flesh has softened and the glaze has become golden.

8. Just as you serve it, spoon on the tofu ginger dressing.

This dressing is perfect to dress a salad of thinly sliced ham, warm halved waxy potatoes, green beans and soft-boiled eggs, or when used on a hot-smoked salmon and watercress salad scattered with toasted pumpkin seeds and cherry tomatoes. It's also good tossed with roast sweet potato or Jerusalem artichokes.

HONEY MUSTARD DRESSING

MAKES ABOUT 200 ml

1½ tbsp runny honey
2 tbsp grain mustard
1 tbsp hot English mustard
2 tbsp lemon juice
100 ml light oil (sunflower, canola or
    light olive oil are good)

Mix the honey and mustards together, mix in the lemon juice, then whisk in the oil. You shouldn't need to add salt.

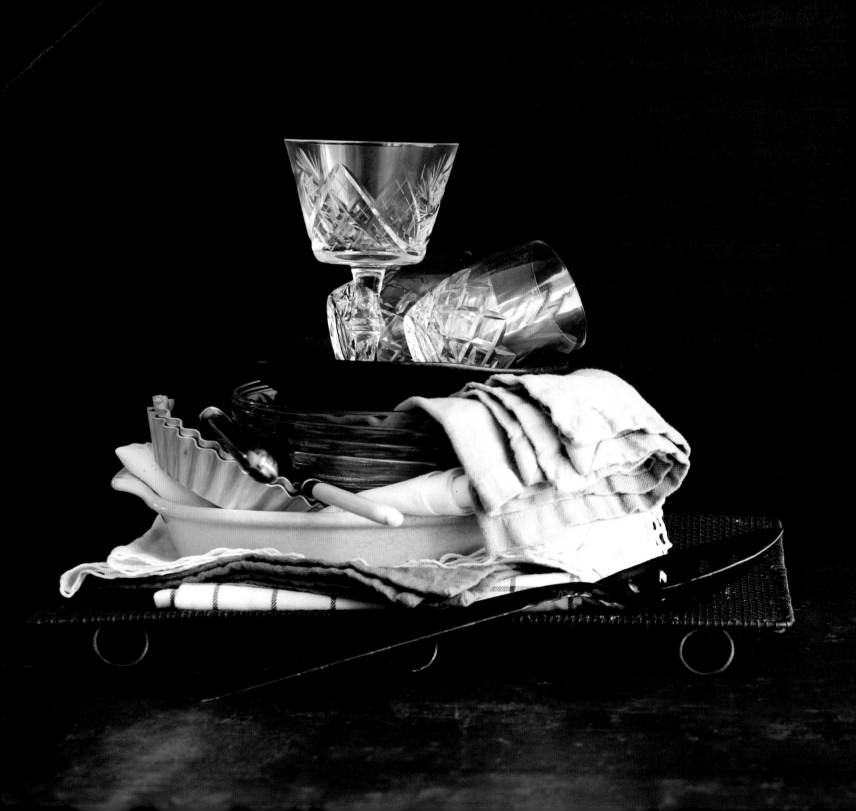

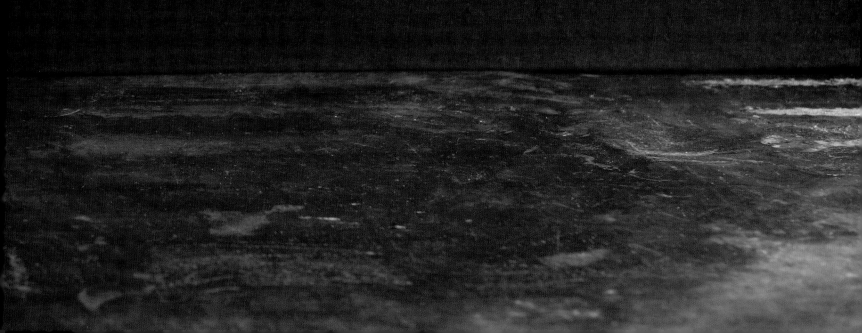

| CHAPTER SEVEN |

TEA TROLLEY AND DESSERTS

Delicious eaten hot or cold, this is terrific served with mixed berries or diced fresh mango and passion fruit. If you don't have coconut milk, use the more traditional single cream.

COCONUT BREAD AND BUTTER PUDDING **FOR 6 DESSERTS**

250 g butter, melted

8 slices slightly stale fruit bread (or plain bread and 2 tbsp dried fruits)

4 tbsp desiccated coconut, lightly toasted

3 eggs

60 g caster sugar

1 tsp finely grated orange zest

½ tsp vanilla extract

350 ml coconut milk

fresh fruit and runny cream or yoghurt, to serve (optional)

1. Preheat oven to 160°C. Butter a baking dish (ideally, 4 slices of bread should fit in the dish in one layer).

2. Butter all 8 slices of bread on both sides and sit 4 in the dish. Sprinkle with half the toasted coconut.

3. Whisk the eggs, sugar, orange zest, vanilla and coconut milk and pour one-third over the bread.

4. Lay on the next 4 slices of bread, sprinkle with the remaining coconut and pour on the remaining egg mixture. Press the bread down gently into the cream mixture.

5. Bake for 20–25 minutes, until the custard has set. Insert a sharp knife or toothpick to check – it shouldn't be too moist.

6. To serve, simply scoop the pudding onto a plate and scatter with fresh fruit, adding runny cream or yoghurt, if you like.

It was the humble crumble that broke down the barrier of snobbery the French held towards British cuisine, when it began appearing on numerous French menus and even in French cookbooks. I think it's hilarious that something so simple met no resistance, but then a crumble is a most satisfying dessert.

APPLE, PRUNE AND PECAN CRUMBLE WITH CARAMEL CREAM SAUCE **FOR 6 DESSERTS**

6 Granny Smith apples (or similar –
   slightly sour and firm)
10 pitted prunes, halved
½ tsp ground cloves
400 g caster sugar
100 g pecans, toasted and roughly
   chopped
80 g unsalted butter, at fridge
   temperature (plus extra for greasing
   the ramekins)
100 g wholemeal flour
2 tbsp water
200 ml apple juice
300 ml cream
1 good pinch salt

1. Preheat oven to 180°C. Lightly butter 6 x 250 ml ramekins (or 1 large ovenproof dish).

2. Remove the core from all the apples. Peel 4 of them, cut into eighths and place in a pot. Coarsely grate the remaining unpeeled apples (the peel adds a sharp edge to the crumble) and add to the pot along with the prunes, cloves and 100 g sugar. Gently bring to a simmer and cook for 10 minutes with a lid on.

3. Divide the apple mixture among the ramekins and scatter the pecans on top.

4. Reserve 10 g butter and rub the remainder into the flour with 100 g sugar until it resembles breadcrumbs, then sprinkle loosely over the top of the apple mixture. Dot the remaining butter on top.

5. Place the ramekins on a baking tray and bake in the middle of the oven until the crumble turns bubbly and golden; about 20 minutes.

6. Meanwhile, make the caramel sauce. Place the remaining sugar in a heavy-based pan with the water and put over a moderate heat. Stir until the sugar dissolves, then turn the heat up – once it begins to boil, don't stir. Cook over a moderate-high heat until it turns a deep caramel colour, then gradually add the apple juice in three lots (it will splatter and steam, so stand back) and bring to a boil. Cook for a few minutes to reduce it to a thick syrup, then add the cream and salt. Bring back to the boil and simmer for a few minutes.

7. To serve, give everyone a crumble and pass the warm sauce around in a jug.

This deliciously spiced flan is very rich and best served a little chilled. You can also bake
it in a pastry case or use a biscuit crumb base.

SPICED PUMPKIN, FIG AND PINE NUT FLAN **FOR 6-8 DESSERTS**

500 g pumpkin, peeled and roughly cut into 2 cm dice

2 tsp mixed spice (or a combination of cinnamon, ginger, cloves, nutmeg and star anise)

100 g soft brown sugar

1 tbsp crystallized or candied stem ginger, chopped

50 g unsalted butter, melted

6 dried figs, stems removed, thinly sliced

100 g pine nuts, lightly toasted

2 egg yolks (or 1 whole egg)

2 lemons

3 tbsp caster sugar

¼ vanilla bean, split open and seeds scraped out (or ¼ tsp vanilla extract)

100 g mascarpone

150 ml cream, straight from the fridge

1. Preheat oven to 170°C. Have a 24–30 cm flan tin to hand.

2. Mix the pumpkin, mixed spice, brown sugar, ginger and butter together in a baking dish lined with baking paper, and bake until just cooked. Test the pumpkin with a knife – it should slide in with little resistance.

3. Mix the sliced figs and pine nuts into the mixture, mashing the pumpkin a little, and leave to sit for 10 minutes.

4. Mix in the egg yolks, then spoon the mixture into the flan tin and bake until golden; about 20–25 minutes. Take from the oven and leave to cool completely, then place in the fridge.

5. Using a potato peeler, peel one of the lemons, avoiding the white pith, and julienne the peel. Juice both lemons and add with the peel to a small pan. Add the caster sugar and bring to a boil, then rapidly simmer until you have a thickish syrup. Tip into a bowl and mix in the vanilla bean seeds or extract, then leave to cool.

6. Stir in the mascarpone, then add the cream and whisk to form almost firm peaks and spread this over the flan.

A simple dessert when served with custard, yoghurt or ice cream, it's also great for breakfast served with granola.

DRIED FRUIT, MAPLE SYRUP AND ALMOND COMPOTE FOR 8-10 DESSERTS

1.5 litres apple or pear juice

150 ml maple syrup or runny honey

15 cm cinnamon quill, snapped into 3–4 pieces

6 cloves

6 allspice, cracked

½ tsp grated nutmeg

1 tbsp grated ginger, fresh or candied

300 g dried figs, stems removed and quartered

300 g dried apricots, thickly sliced

200 g currants, sultanas, raisins or a mixture of all 3

200 g whole almonds, toasted

1. Place the juice, syrup or honey, spices and ginger in a large pan and bring to a boil.

2. Add the dried fruit and almonds and bring back the boil, stirring as it approaches boiling point. Put a lid on the pan and simmer for 10 minutes, then turn the heat off and leave the mixture to rest in a warm place, such as the back of the stove, for 1 hour.

3. If the compote is a little dry, top it up with more juice or hot water. Serve warm or straight from the fridge, depending on the season.

This rippled sorbet really is easy to make even without an ice cream machine. I didn't have one when I made it. Just make sure you have your terrine mould already chilled in the freezer before you make it. You can replace the raspberry purée with any other puréed fruit, such as mango, peach or blackberry.

RASPBERRY SORBET WITH HONEY CREAM RIPPLE **FOR 8–10 DESSERTS**

600 g raspberries, plus extra for serving
200 g caster sugar
4 tbsp lemon or lime juice
150 ml honey
300 ml cream

1. Line a 1.5 litre terrine tin with a double layer of plastic wrap and place in the freezer.

2. Purée the raspberries, sugar, lemon or lime juice and 50 ml honey in a blender or food processor until fine. You can strain this if you want, but some seeds left in give it a good texture.

3. Place in an ice cream machine and churn until frozen. Alternatively, freeze in a shallow metal tray, stirring every 30 minutes with a fork, until almost frozen. The stirring prevents ice crystals forming as it freezes, which helps make a smoother sorbet.

4. Once frozen, in a large chilled bowl whisk the cream with the remaining honey to form almost firm peaks. Add the sorbet to the same bowl and, using just 5–6 movements, fold the sorbet through the cream, making sure the sorbet and cream don't become incorporated (see opposite).

5. Tip the mixture into the terrine and fold extra plastic wrap over the top to tightly seal it. Freeze for at least 8 hours.

6. To serve, peel the plastic wrap from the top of the terrine, invert onto a platter and tip out. Remove the rest of the plastic wrap and thickly slice. Serve with fresh raspberries.

So called, as far as I'm concerned, because they are so easy to knock up, fools are surprisingly light to eat and all you need serve with them are thin biscotti or a meringue. I like to make mine with sheep's or goat's yoghurt for a lighter finish, and New Zealand manuka honey adds a lovely background intensity.

RASPBERRY HONEY FOOL **FOR 6 DESSERTS**

300 g raspberries
2 tbsp icing sugar
2 tbsp lemon or lime juice
300 ml cream
250 ml plain yoghurt
50 ml honey

1. Mix the raspberries with the icing sugar and lemon or lime juice and leave to sit in the fridge for 20 minutes.

2. Whip the cream, yoghurt and honey in a bowl to medium-firm peaks.

3. Divide half the berries between six glasses, then gently fold the remaining berries into the whipped cream. Spoon this over the berries and return to the fridge.

4. Leave to rest for 20 minutes before serving.

The fruity tropical flavours are enhanced by the texture of the gingernuts. Make sure you eat this soon after you've made it, before the biscuits lose their crunch.

PASSION FRUIT, MANGO AND GINGERNUT FOOL **FOR 4 DESSERTS**

1 mango
200 ml cream
200 ml crème fraîche
1 heaped tbsp brown sugar
4 gingernuts, roughly crushed
3 passion fruit, pulp removed

1. Peel the mango and cut into chunks, then divide among four glasses.

2. Whip the cream, crème fraîche and sugar together to medium peaks, then fold in the gingernuts and one-third of the passion fruit pulp. Spoon this on top of the mango and spoon the remaining passion fruit on top.

3. Leave in the fridge for no more than 1 hour, then serve.

*These creamy fruity trifles are easy to knock up and look gorgeous when served in a
fancy old glass. Any berry can replace the strawberries and any ripe fruit the peaches.
For adults, I'd add a few good slugs of sweet sherry to the cream!*

SUPER-QUICK STRAWBERRY AND PEACH 'NOT QUITE' TRIFLES
FOR 4-6 DESSERTS

150 ml cream
2 tbsp caster sugar
1 tsp vanilla extract
200 ml thick plain yoghurt
250 g strawberries, hulled
6 slices firm sponge cake or light pound
  cake
2 ripe peaches
icing sugar, for dusting

1. Whip the cream, sugar and vanilla until soft peaks, then beat in the yoghurt until quite firm.

2. Place a tablespoon of the mixture into the bottom of each of 4–6 glasses.

3. Purée three-quarters of the strawberries and spoon half of the purée on top of the cream.

4. Cut the cake into 1–2 cm cubes and sit on the purée, gently pressing them in.

5. Spoon on the remaining purée.

6. Cut the peaches in half, remove the stones and cut into chunks.

7. Divide the peaches among the glasses and top with the remaining cream. Place in the fridge to firm up for at least 2 hours.

8. To serve, slice the remaining strawberries and lay on top, then dust with icing sugar.

Membrillo *is the Spanish word for quince paste, or what the Italians call* cotognata. *I use it here teamed up with dark chocolate and PX (Pedro Ximenez sherry) – the most delicious, rich sweet sherry imaginable – which is also incredible served simply drizzled over vanilla ice cream.*

CHOCOLATE GANACHE AND MEMBRILLO TART WITH PX CREAM

MAKES 4 x 10 cm TARTS

1 recipe Spanish-style Sweet Short Crust Pastry (see page 245)
200 g dark chocolate (60–80% cocoa solids)
270 g cream, at fridge temperature
150 g membrillo, cut into 1 cm dice
50 ml PX sherry or port
50 g hazelnuts, toasted, peeled and roughly crushed

1. Line four 10 cm tart tins with sweet short crust pastry and fully blind bake (see page 245).

2. Make the chocolate ganache by melting the chocolate in a metal bowl over simmering water (or microwave it in bursts).

3. Stir in 120 ml of the cream to form a smooth consistency, then leave to firm up for 15 minutes. Divide half the ganache among the tart shells and poke the membrillo chunks in.

4. Put the remaining ganache into a piping bag and pipe patterns over the membrillo, or simply dollop it on and flatten it out as best you can. The tarts will keep like this for up to 8 hours if kept airtight.

5. Beat the PX and cream together until soft peaks form.

6. To serve, place a tart on each plate, dollop on a large mound of the remaining cream and scatter with the hazelnuts, then eat straight away.

SPANISH-STYLE SWEET SHORT CRUST PASTRY MAKES 750 g

400 g flour
100 g icing sugar
210 g unsalted butter, from the freezer,
  cut into 2 cm dice
½ egg yolk (I know this sounds odd but
  you don't need a whole yolk)
2 tbsp dry sherry (water, or even vodka
  or grappa will do)

1. Sift the flour and sugar together and then rub in the butter with your fingers (or use a food processor).

2. Lightly beat the half yolk with the sherry, then mix into the flour. Don't overwork it as it will tighten the pastry. If it needs more moisture, just add a little more sherry.

3. Once it has come together as a dough, place in a plastic bag in the fridge for 1 hour.

4. Roll out to 4 mm thick on a lightly floured board and use to line your tart tin (or tins).

5. Line with scrunched-up baking paper and fill with baking beans. Rest in the fridge for 30 minutes, then blind bake at 180°C until golden, about 20 minutes.

6. For the Chocolate Ganache and Membrillo Tart with PX Cream (see page 244), the pastry needs to be fully baked, so then remove the beans and baking paper and continue to cook until golden brown.

I love rhubarb and it's fairly easy to grow in most gardens, so great to have around. Remember that it's very sour so needs quite a bit of sugar added when cooking. It can be easily stewed in a pan, but by baking it you get to see the lovely stalks in their natural state.

BAKED RHUBARB WITH GINGER AND CINNAMON **FOR 4 DESSERTS**

500 g rhubarb stalks, cut into 10 cm lengths (choose stalks that aren't too fat or old as they can be a little too stringy)

150 ml orange or apple juice

1 thumb ginger, peeled and julienned

1 x 10 cm cinnamon quill, snapped into 4 pieces

150 g caster sugar

100 ml water

cream, ice cream, yoghurt or custard, to serve

1. Preheat oven to 180°C.

2. Place the rhubarb in a non-reactive baking dish large enough to hold it in one layer.

3. Place the remaining ingredients in a saucepan and bring to the boil. Put a lid on and simmer for 15 minutes to allow the cinnamon to infuse into the syrup.

4. Pour the syrup and spices over the rhubarb, then bake until the rhubarb is just beginning to soften; about 20–30 minutes. You should be able to just squeeze the rhubarb between your fingers, although you want to have a little resistance.

5. You can serve it straight from the oven or at room temperature with cream, ice cream, yoghurt or custard.

The rose sugar will last for a month if kept airtight in a dark place. A cartouche is a disc of baking paper cut to the same diameter as the inside of the pot. Use a pot lid as a template, and cut a small X in the centre to let out steam. The pears can be eaten hot or cold.

STAR ANISE AND RED WINE-POACHED PEARS WITH ROSE PETAL CREAM FOR 6 DESSERTS

1 bottle red wine (choose one with a deep colour and a little spice – a syrah or chianti would work well)

6 star anise

125 ml runny honey

2 bay leaves

450 g sugar

1 litre water

6 pears suitable for cooking (firm ones work best)

20 g dried rose petals (make sure they're edible and aromatic)

200 ml cream

1 tbsp natural rose-water

1. Place the wine, star anise, honey, bay leaves and 300 g sugar in a pot large enough to hold the pears comfortably. Add the water and bring to the boil, then simmer for 15 minutes.

2. Peel strips of skin from the pears and remove their cores.

3. Add them to the simmering red wine and bring back to the boil. Top up with boiling water if they're not covered, then sit a cartouche on top of the pears, turn to a rapid simmer and cook for 40–50 minutes until a skewer goes through the flesh easily. Pears are best cooked beyond crunchy – by cooking longer than you might think, they take on a lovely texture.

4. Meanwhile, make the rose sugar. Place the petals and the reserved sugar in a food processor and blitz for 30 seconds, scraping the sides down several times.

5. Whip 4 tbsp rose sugar, the cream and the rose-water together to medium peaks, then cover and place in the fridge.

6. To serve, sit a pear on a plate, spoon on some of the poaching liquid, dollop on some cream and sprinkle with a little extra rose sugar.

This is very much a 'small portion' dessert as the chocolate is really rich and full-on. If you don't enjoy coffee in your desserts, you can use spices instead, such as cardamom, cloves, cinnamon and even dried chilli flakes for a Mexican feel. The Cinnamon Shortbread (see page 252) goes really well with it, too.

CHOCOLATE MOCHA POTS WITH CINNAMON SHORTBREAD **FOR 6-8 DESSERTS**

280 g milk

250 g cream

2 tsp espresso coffee grounds (the grains, not an actual espresso) or instant coffee

100 g caster sugar (plus 1 tsp for the whipped cream)

4 egg yolks

200 g dark chocolate (60–80% cocoa solids), roughly chopped

1. It may seem a little odd weighing the wet ingredients – but it will make it far more accurate. Place the milk, 150 g cream, the ground coffee and 50 g sugar in a saucepan and slowly bring to a simmer, stirring frequently, then turn the heat off. Put the lid on the pot and leave to infuse for 10 minutes.

2. Take the lid off and slowly bring back to a simmer, stirring gently as you do.

3. Whisk the yolks for 1 minute with the remaining sugar. When the milk has come back to heat, carefully whisk one-third of it into the yolks, then pour back into the pan.

4. Stir over a moderate heat until the custard coats the back of the spoon; around 3–4 minutes.

5. Take off the heat and whisk in the chocolate until it's incorporated, then pour through a fine sieve (to remove the coffee grounds) into a clean jug. Pour into glasses or ramekins and place on a tray in the fridge. Once cooled, seal tightly with plastic wrap and leave for at least 4 hours.

6. To serve, lightly whip the remaining 100 g cream with 1 tsp sugar and dollop on top. Serve with a cinnamon shortbread or two (see page 252).

CINNAMON SHORTBREAD MAKES 20-30 BISCUITS

250 g unsalted butter, at room
   temperature
160 g caster sugar
250 g flour
130 g cornflour
2 tsp ground cinnamon
1 pinch salt

1. Preheat oven to 170°C. Line a baking tray with baking paper.

2. Cream the butter and sugar together.

3. Sift together the flour, cornflour, cinnamon and salt. Mix into the creamed mixture gently until you form a dough – don't overwork or it will produce tough biscuits.

4. Tip the dough onto the baking tray and, using a rolling pin or your hands, form a rectangle about 1 cm thick. Cut with a sharp knife into fingers or squares.

5. Bake for 20–24 minutes until golden.

6. Take from the oven and cut them again where you already have – they will have swollen a bit. Leave to cool on the tray for 5 minutes, then transfer carefully to a cake rack. Store in an airtight container.

Pasties are easier to make than pies as you don't need to line a tart shell. Use bought pastry, but do try to find one with a high percentage of butter, rather than margarine, as it will taste much better. Serve these warm with runny cream or vanilla ice cream.

SPICED BANANA, PECAN, CHOCOLATE AND MAPLE SYRUP PASTIES
MAKES 4 PASTIES

600 g puff pastry
50 g unsalted butter
4 tbsp maple syrup or runny honey
1 tsp ground cinnamon
½ tsp ground ginger
1 small pinch cayenne pepper or
  paprika
3 bananas, peeled and cut into 1 cm
  slices
100 g pecan nuts, lightly toasted and
  roughly chopped
1 egg, beaten, for egg-wash
1 pinch salt
100 g dark chocolate (60–80% cocoa
  solids), roughly chopped
caster sugar, for sprinkling

1. Preheat oven to 200°C. Line a baking tray with baking paper.

2. Roll out the pastry to 4 mm thick and cut four discs about 18 cm in diameter.

3. Heat up a wide pan, add the butter and cook until it goes a nut-brown colour, shaking the pan as it heats up.

4. Add the maple syrup and spices and bring to a sizzle, then add the banana slices and gently cook them for 4 minutes over a moderate heat. They will turn to mush if overcooked or stirred too much, so go gently.

5. Mix in the pecans, tip into a bowl and leave to completely cool.

6. Beat the egg with the salt and brush it around the outside edges of the pastry discs. Divide the banana among the centres of the pastry discs, then sprinkle on the chocolate. Fold one side of the pastry over the filling to give you a pasty shape, pressing the edges together firmly with a fork dipped in flour, expelling any air pockets.

7. Brush the pasties with egg-wash and sprinkle generously with the sugar.

8. Place on the baking tray and bake in the centre of the oven for 30 minutes, or until the pasties have gone a lovely dark golden colour.

The two components in this dessert, the curd and the jelly, are really versatile and, combined, they make a lovely light dessert. Use the jelly to top a summer berry trifle, and the orange curd to fill small tart cases topped with a chocolate ganache. You will have more curd than you need, but it keeps covered in the fridge for a week.

LAYERED ORANGE CURD, YOGHURT AND WATERMELON JELLY WITH ALMONDS

MAKES 6 x 200 ml GLASSES OR 1 LARGE DISH

2 juicy oranges

90 g white sugar

2 large eggs

3 egg yolks

140 g unsalted butter, cut into 1 cm dice, taken from the fridge 30 minutes before using

1 tbsp orange blossom water or rose-water

180 ml plain yoghurt (I prefer ewe's milk yoghurt as it's good and tangy)

700 g watermelon flesh, deseeded (it must be ripe)

4 leaves gelatine

2 tbsp boiling water

50 g flaked almonds, toasted

1. First make the orange curd. Grate the zest from the oranges and place in a bowl. Squeeze the juice (you need 170 ml) and add to the zest along with the sugar, whole eggs and egg yolks. Whisk thoroughly, then pour into a heavy-based pan and cook over a moderate heat, stirring constantly, until it begins to thicken; about 3–4 minutes. Don't let it boil at any stage or you'll curdle the eggs.

2. Turn the heat to low, then start adding the butter. Whisk in two lumps initially until they are almost absorbed, then add one lump at a time and continue until all the butter has been absorbed. Cook for another 20 seconds, whisking continuously, then take off the heat and whisk in the orange blossom water or rose-water.

3. Spoon 2–3 tbsp curd into each glass (depending on their size) and leave to cool, then place in the fridge to firm up for at least 1 hour. Spoon the yoghurt on top and return to the fridge.

4. Make the jelly. Cut the watermelon into chunks, place in a blender, juice extractor or food processor and purée. Pass through a sieve to remove the fibre, then measure out 500 ml. Soak the gelatine in cold water for 5 minutes, then drain it and place in a bowl. Add the boiling water to the gelatine and mix to dissolve, then stir in the watermelon purée until thoroughly combined. Place the bowl of jelly in an ice bath (another larger bowl half filled with iced water) and when it begins to set spoon it over the yoghurt in the glasses, then place in the fridge to fully set.

5. To serve, scatter the almonds over the jelly.

For some reason, whenever I use peanuts in a biscuit I feel they should be called a cookie – it must be due to watching episodes of The Partridge Family *and* The Brady Bunch *on TV when I was much younger. If you don't have peanuts to hand, you can use chunky peanut butter instead and avoid the second step.*

PEANUT, PECAN AND CHOCOLATE COOKIES **MAKES 20 COOKIES**

100 g peanuts, unsalted, toasted and
   skins off
100 g butter, diced
100 g brown sugar
1 large egg
100 g flour
½ tsp baking powder
½ tsp baking soda
60 g pecans, toasted and roughly
   chopped
60 g demerara sugar
50 g chocolate (milk chocolate or darker
  – it's up to you)

1. Preheat oven to 190°C. Line two baking trays with baking paper.

2. Blitz the peanuts to a fine crumb in a food processor.

3. Add the butter and sugar and process for 30 seconds, scraping the sides down twice. Add the egg and blitz for a further 20 seconds. Sift in the flour, baking powder and baking soda and pulse to combine, then tip into a bowl and mix in the pecans.

4. Divide the dough into four, then each quarter into five even-sized pieces and roll into balls. Toss the balls in the demerara sugar to lightly coat them; a shallow bowl works well for this. Place 10 cookies on each baking tray, giving them plenty of room to spread, then lightly press down with your fingers and bake for 10–12 minutes until they have a crust on top.

5. Take the trays from the oven and gently but firmly bang them on the bench twice – don't ask why, but it helps keep them in shape. Leave to cool on the trays for a few minutes before cooling on cake racks.

6. Melt the chocolate, then drizzle it over the cookies in a random or defined pattern and leave to set before eating.

This very simple dessert makes a terrific light end to a summer lunch or dinner and can be served as simply as in the photo opposite. Alternatively, it can be served with runny cream and biscotti, or scooped from a larger bowl and served with ice cream or a meringue.

STRAWBERRY AND GINGER-BEER JELLIES **MAKES 8 SMALL JELLIES OR 1 LARGE ONE**

6 leaves gelatine (or 1 tbsp powdered gelatine)

250 ml apple juice

2 tbsp lemon juice

⅓ vanilla bean, split open and seeds scraped out (or ¼ tsp pure vanilla extract)

400 ml ginger beer

12 large ripe strawberries, hulled and cut into thin wedges

1. If using powdered gelatine, sprinkle it over 50 ml of the apple juice and stir well.

2. Place the remaining apple juice, lemon juice and the vanilla bean and its seeds in a saucepan and bring to a simmer, then turn off the heat.

3. Soak the leaf gelatine in 1 litre very cold water, placing them in one at a time and leaving for a few minutes to soften. Drain the gelatine of excess water, very gently squeezing the sheets.

4. Add the soaked gelatine leaves (or powdered gelatine mix) to the warm apple juice, stir to dissolve, then tip into a jug and stir in the ginger beer.

5. Divide the strawberry pieces among eight small glasses or place in one large bowl. Pour on the jelly mixture, cover tightly with plastic wrap and leave to set in the fridge for about 4–6 hours.

You can make either one large tart or six individual smaller ones. They're great eaten straight from the oven, but are also lovely served at room temperature with whipped cream or ice cream. Use fresh cherries in season, but otherwise canned, bottled or frozen will work – just make sure they're pitted and drained.

CHERRY OAT CRUMBLE TARTS

MAKES 6 x 10 cm TARTS OR 1 x 30 cm TART

1 recipe Spanish-style Sweet Short Crust
    Pastry (see page 245)
140 g butter
150 g flour
½ tsp baking powder
60 g demerara sugar
40 g rolled oats (smaller oats work best)
250 g pitted cherries
2 tbsp runny honey

1. Preheat oven to 180°C. Line six 10 cm fluted tart tins or one 30 cm fluted tart tin with short crust pastry – don't blind bake.

2. Using either your fingers or a food processor, rub the butter into the flour and baking powder. Mix in the demerara sugar and oats. Divide two-thirds of the mixture between the tart shells.

3. Mix the cherries and honey together and spoon into the tart shells, then sprinkle with the remaining crumble.

4. Bake on a tray in the centre of the oven for 20–30 minutes until the pastry is golden and the crumble has cooked.

*While vol-au-vents seem to have been relegated to the 'bad wedding catering memories'
league, they do in fact serve a unique and much forgotten culinary purpose: to hold
saucy foods in place. You will get a lot of leftover pastry when making them (from
cutting the rims), so you could roll that out and make some cheese straws or the like.*

TOFFEED PINEAPPLE AND MARMALADE MASCARPONE VOL-AU-VENTS **FOR 4 DESSERTS**

450 g puff pastry
1 egg white, lightly beaten
2 tsp brown sugar
50 g butter
80 g caster sugar
½ pineapple, peeled, core removed,
    flesh cut into 2 cm chunks
150 ml cream
100 g mascarpone
2 tbsp fine cut marmalade or apricot
    jam
1 tbsp brandy or rum (optional)

1. Roll the pastry out to a rectangle roughly 45 cm x 22 cm. Use an 11 cm pastry cutter to cut eight discs, then take four of the discs and cut the centres out using an 8 cm cutter. You'll now have four discs and four rims. Place the discs on a baking tray lined with baking paper and brush with the egg white, sit the rims on top and brush with more egg white. Use a fork to prick the bases a dozen times, then sprinkle the brown sugar around the rims and the bases. Place in the fridge for 20 minutes.

2. Preheat oven to 220°C. Bake the vol-au-vents in the top of the oven for 18–25 minutes, when they will have risen up and become golden. After 12 minutes, take from the oven briefly and press the centre down with the back of a spoon to collapse the puffing pastry.

3. Meanwhile, in a wide pan, cook the butter over moderate heat until it turns nut-brown. Sprinkle in the caster sugar and cook to caramelize it, stirring gently.

4. Add the pineapple, which will make the sugar seize up, but keep it cooking and eventually it will soften again. Place a lid on the pan and continue to cook the pineapple until you can easily poke a skewer through it.

5. Take the lid off, add the cream and rapidly simmer for 8–10 minutes to reduce the liquid by half.

6. Mix the mascarpone with the marmalade and brandy or rum (if using). To serve, dollop the mascarpone into the base of the vol-au-vents, and spoon the hot pineapple and cooking juices on top.

*These puddings may look like a lot of fuss, but they're fairly simple – just read the recipe
thoroughly in advance and have your ramekins prepped. Serve them straight from the
oven, or make them up to three days ahead then reheat in a microwave on full heat for
1–1½ minutes or cover loosely with foil and place in an oven at 180°C for 10 minutes.*

STICKY BANANA ESPRESSO PUDDING WITH MAPLE SYRUP CREAM **FOR 10 DESSERTS**

140 g soft butter (plus extra for
 buttering the moulds)
90 g demerara sugar or soft brown
 sugar (plus extra for preparing the
 ramekins)
50 g caster sugar
300 g ripe bananas (2–3 bananas),
 peeled and sliced 1 cm thick
1 egg
1 tsp vanilla extract
1 double espresso (or 50 ml strong
 instant coffee)
320 g flour
2 tsp baking powder
10 fresh Medjool dates or dried dates,
 pitted and cut into 6
150 ml water
½ tsp baking soda
300 ml cream
2 tbsp maple syrup

1. Preheat oven to 180°C. Brush 10 x 250 ml ramekins thickly with a few tablespoons of extra butter and coat with extra demerara sugar, then place the moulds in the fridge.

2. Cream the butter, demerara sugar and caster sugar together, beating in half the sliced bananas as you go. Beat the egg, vanilla and espresso together, then whisk it into the creamed mixture – don't worry if it separates as it'll all come back together.

3. Sift the flour and baking powder and mix into the batter.

4. Put the dates, the remaining banana slices and the water in a saucepan. Slowly bring to the boil, then take off the heat. Stir in the baking soda (it will froth up a little), then mix thoroughly into the dough.

5. Divide the mixture among the moulds and sprinkle with a little demerara sugar.

6. Place the ramekins on a baking tray and bake in the centre of the oven for 20 minutes. Test with a skewer to see if they're cooked; they need to be a little gooey in the middle. While they're cooking, lightly whip the cream and maple syrup together until soft peaks form.

7. If you're serving these straight away, be careful unmoulding them as they will be very hot. Run a knife around the lip of the ramekin; then, using a tea towel to hold them, invert onto a plate and serve with the cream. Alternatively, if you're making them in advance, leave them to cool for 10 minutes before unmoulding.

Quinces require just one thing – to be cooked gently and for a long time. If you have any quince left over, it goes well with roast chicken, pork or duck, and it's also lovely in salads or as the fruit base for a crumble. Serve this cold or warm, as it is or with whipped cream, yoghurt or custard.

SAFFRON-BRAISED QUINCE WITH RHUBARB **FOR 6-8 DESSERTS**

600 ml water
300 ml sweet dessert wine or apple or
  pear juice
4 allspice, crushed
1 generous pinch saffron
400 g caster sugar
4 large quince
200 g rhubarb, cut into 1 cm lengths

1. Preheat oven to 170°C. Place the water, wine or juice, allspice, saffron and 300 g sugar in a pot and bring to a boil, then simmer for 5 minutes.

2. Meanwhile, peel the quince (wear gloves as they leave a sticky film on your hands), cut into halves, remove cores and seeds (but keep the cores along with the peel of 1 quince) and cut each half into four wedges. Place prepared quince in a bowl of cold water as you go – it will discolour, but this will disappear when cooking.

3. Wrap the reserved cores and the peel in a piece of muslin or cotton, tie it up loosely and add to the simmering liquid – it all adds texture and body to the quince.

4. Once the poaching liquor is ready, place drained quince wedges in a ceramic or stainless steel roasting dish in a single layer. Carefully pour the unstrained liquid over. You want them almost submerged – top up with boiling water if necessary. Place a sheet of baking paper on top of the quince, then seal tightly with foil. Bake in the centre of the oven for 1¾ hours. Remove the dish from the oven, pour off 250 ml of the cooking juices, and leave the quince to cool.

5. In a wide pan, cook the remaining 100 g sugar over a moderate heat until it caramelizes, shaking the pan as the sugar melts. Once it's turned a caramel colour, pour in 250 ml of the quince cooking liquid and bring to a boil to dissolve the caramel. Add the rhubarb and gently poach it over a rapid simmer until the rhubarb has softened – don't let it overcook, as it'll become mushy. Leave to cool.

6. To serve, spoon quince and rhubarb into your plates and drizzle with their cooking liquors.

Saffron and butternut (or pumpkin or sweet potato) go so well together – not only in soups and the like but also in desserts, especially when teamed with spices and cream. These little baked custard pots can also be made as one large flan, and if you have a brûlée torch you can sprinkle them with sugar and blast with heat to make a toffeed brûlée top.

BAKED SAFFRON, BUTTERNUT AND GINGERNUT CUSTARD POTS **FOR 6 DESSERTS**

6 gingernuts (or similar hard spiced biscuit), coarsely crushed

500 g butternut, peeled, deseeded and diced

30 g unsalted butter

150 ml cream

80 g caster or soft brown sugar

¼ tsp ground cloves

¼ tsp ground cardamom

½ tsp ground cinnamon

1 small pinch saffron

50 ml crème fraîche

½ tsp vanilla extract

4 egg yolks

runny cream or extra crème fraîche, to serve

1. Preheat oven to 160°C. Divide the crushed gingernuts between six 200 ml ovenproof ramekins and place on a baking tray.

2. Put the butternut, butter and cream in a pot and slowly bring to a boil.

3. Stir in the sugar, spices and saffron, place a lid on and simmer until the butternut is cooked.

4. Mash it and push through a sieve, or blend with a stick blender, until smooth.

5. Mix in the crème fraîche, vanilla and egg yolks, then spoon on top of the gingernuts in the ramekins.

6. Bake in the centre of the oven for 15–20 minutes, until the top feels firm and a toothpick inserted comes out relatively clean.

7. Take from the oven and leave to cool, then cover with plastic wrap and place in the fridge for at least 3 hours.

8. To serve, drizzle with runny cream or dollop on some extra crème fraîche.

This is a typical American dessert that you'll be familiar with from television shows from the '70s – but, in reality, shortcake is simply a very light scone.

PEPPERED STRAWBERRY, BASIL AND BLACKBERRY SHORTCAKE **FOR 8 DESSERTS**

225 g flour

3 tbsp caster sugar

1 tbsp baking powder

1 pinch salt

80 g butter, from the fridge, diced

180 ml buttermilk or runny plain yoghurt

1 large handful strawberries, hulled

50 g icing sugar

10 basil leaves, shredded

¼ tsp freshly ground coarse black pepper

1 large handful blackberries or boysenberries

300 ml cream

100 ml thick yoghurt

1. Preheat oven to 220°C. Line a baking tray with baking paper.

2. Sift together the flour, caster sugar, baking powder and salt. Either rub the butter in with your fingers or pulse in a food processor to resemble crumbs. Mix in the buttermilk or yoghurt, then gently knead for 10 seconds. Roll out on a lightly floured board to 2 cm thick and cut into eight pieces of whatever shape you want. Place ½ cm apart on the baking tray and bake for 18–22 minutes. The tops should be golden and the shortcake will have risen just like scones. Take from the oven and leave to cool on a rack.

3. While they're cooking, slice the strawberries and toss with all but 2 tbsp icing sugar, the basil, pepper and berries, then put to one side.

4. Whip the cream with the yoghurt and the remaining icing sugar and put in the fridge.

5. To serve, split the shortcakes in half and spoon three-quarters of the fruit on the bottom halves. Dollop on the cream, then drizzle the berry juices and remaining fruit over that. Sit the shortcake top on and eat immediately.

Panna cotta is one of the great gifts from the Italian pastry kitchen (along with tiramisu), and over the years I have made, and eaten, all sorts of flavours from simple vanilla through to beetroot (the latter wasn't a good idea, I have to say). When blackberries are out of season use strawberries, raspberries or blueberries.

PANNA COTTA WITH BALSAMIC BLACKBERRIES **FOR 6 DESSERTS**

300 ml milk

400 ml cream

½ vanilla bean, split lengthways and seeds scraped out (or 1 tsp pure vanilla extract)

1 x 400 g tin condensed milk

6 leaves gelatine (or 1 tbsp powdered gelatine)

60 g caster sugar

1 tbsp water

100 g blackberries

1 tbsp balsamic vinegar

1. Slowly bring the milk, cream, vanilla bean and scrapings and the condensed milk almost to boiling point, whisking occasionally as it heats up, then turn the heat off and leave for a few minutes.

2. Soak the leaf gelatine in very cold water for 5 minutes. Drain it, gently squeezing out excess water, and stir it into the hot cream (if using powdered gelatine, sprinkle it over 2 tbsp cold water and stir till dissolved, then mix into the hot cream).

3. Strain the mixture through a sieve (or simply remove the vanilla bean) and pour the mixture into six 200 ml dariole moulds.

4. Leave to cool to room temperature, then cover tightly and place in the fridge to set for at least 8 hours.

5. Put the sugar in a saucepan with the water, place over moderate heat and stir until the sugar dissolves, then without stirring, cook until it colours a light caramel. Turn the heat down, add the blackberries and the balsamic (be careful as it will create hot steam) and cook until some of the berries collapse into the caramel, mashing a few with a spoon as they cook. Take off the heat and leave to cool.

6. To serve, dip each mould into a bowl of hot water for a few seconds, then invert onto the centre of a plate and shake gently to release the panna cotta. Spoon the berries and their juices on top and around.

I love banana fritters – they remind me of the Chinese restaurant we had in my home town of Whanganui. Over the years I've eaten them throughout South-East Asia on the roadside in Thailand, in the markets of Singapore and on the beaches in Bali and Malaysia. The addition of the chillied mango sauce is my idea – and I think it's inspired!

BANANA CINNAMON FRITTERS WITH MANGO CHILLI SAUCE **FOR 4-6 DESSERTS**

100 g flour (plus 30 g for dusting)

30 g cornflour

2 pinches salt

2 tbsp caster sugar (plus extra for dusting)

200 ml beer

1 tsp sesame seeds

1 egg white

1 lime

1 ripe mango, peeled and the flesh cut from the stone

¼ red chilli (more or less to taste), seeds intact, finely chopped

vegetable oil, for deep-frying

3–4 bananas

1 tbsp ground cinnamon

1. Sift the flours, salt and caster sugar into a bowl. Make a well in the centre, pour in the beer, then whisk it in starting from the centre, until well combined and without any lumps. Whisk in the sesame seeds and egg white, then place to one side to rest.

2. Grate the zest from the lime and juice it. Place in a blender with the mango flesh and chilli and purée until smooth.

3. Heat the oil to 180°C.

4. Peel the bananas and slice each one on an angle into eight thickish pieces. Mix the 30 g reserved flour with the cinnamon and dust the pieces in it. Place on a plate.

5. Give the batter a stir – it should be a good coating consistency; if it's too thick, mix in a little water. Add 6–8 slices of banana to the batter at a time, then using a fork or tongs drain off excess batter. Deep-fry until golden, keeping them separate as they cook and turning over after 2 minutes to make sure both sides cook evenly.

6. Drain on kitchen paper and dust with the reserved sugar while you cook the remainder.

7. Serve the mango sauce in a ramekin to the side, or simply spoon it over the hot bananas.

The sultanas in this recipe stay nice and chewy when baked and make a great contrast to the buttery biscuit.

SULTANA AND FIVE-SPICE SHORTBREAD **MAKES 20 BISCUITS**

280 g unsalted butter, at room
 temperature
180 g caster sugar (plus 2 tbsp for
 sprinkling)
2 tsp ground five-spice or allspice
80 g sultanas
120 g rice flour
100 g wholemeal flour
160 g white flour

1. Preheat oven to 180°C. Line a baking tray with baking paper.

2. Place the butter, sugar and five-spice or allspice in a food processor and blitz for 5 seconds. Scrape the sides of the processor down, then blitz again.

3. Add the sultanas and flours and blitz to just bring the dough together. Tip onto a bench and gently knead for a few seconds.

4. Take pieces of the dough, whatever size you want, and roll into balls. Press flat with your fingers or a fork on the baking tray.

5. Sprinkle each biscuit with the remaining 2 tbsp sugar, then leave to rest in the fridge for 10 minutes.

6. Bake until golden; around 14–18 minutes.

7. Once done, remove from the oven and leave to cool on the tray for a few minutes, before transferring to a cake rack to cool completely. Store in an airtight jar.

These tarts rely on the best blueberries available – they need to be plump and flavoursome.

BLUEBERRY CUSTARD TARTS
MAKES 4 x 10–12 cm TARTS OR 1 x 24 cm TART

300 g Spanish-style Sweet Short Crust
Pastry (see page 245), rolled out 5 mm
thick
4 egg yolks
40 g icing sugar (plus extra for dusting
the tarts)
160 ml cream
½ tsp vanilla extract
200 g blueberries
cream or crème fraîche, to serve

1. Preheat oven to 180°C.

2. Line four 10–12 cm fluted tart tins or one 24 cm tart tin with the pastry and rest in the fridge for 20 minutes. Line with baking paper, fill with baking beans, then blind bake on a baking tray until the pastry rim is golden.

3. Carefully remove the lining and beans and bake another 5 minutes, by which time the pastry should be golden all over.

4. Whisk the egg yolks and icing sugar for 20 seconds, then mix in the cream and vanilla.

5. Divide the blueberries among the tart shells, then pour on the cream mixture and return to the oven, dropping the temperature to 160°C.

6. Bake for 30 minutes, at which point the custard should just be set. If it isn't, bake until it is. Take from the oven and leave to cool on the tray, then carefully remove from the tart tins.

7. To serve, dust with icing sugar and serve with either runny or lightly whipped cream or crème fraîche.

The combination of olive oil and chocolate is lovely and well worth trying – even if it sounds a bit odd. Don't cook these too much – you want the mousse to be a bit gooey. If you're not a fan of marmalade, replace it with some poached pears, apple, quince or rhubarb.

WARM CHOCOLATE OLIVE OIL MOUSSE AND MARMALADE TARTS

MAKES 6 x 12 cm TARTS OR 1 x 30 cm TART

6 pre-baked cocoa pastry tart shells (see page 273)
200 g marmalade (not too coarse)
240 g dark chocolate (60–80% cocoa solids), chopped or coarsely grated
3 tbsp extra virgin olive oil
5 eggs
¼ cup icing sugar, sifted
cream, crème fraîche or ice cream, to serve

1. Preheat oven to 190°C.

2. Spoon the marmalade into your pre-baked tart shells.

3. Melt the chocolate and olive oil in a microwave or over a double boiler.

4. Separate the eggs and beat the whites to firm peaks with the icing sugar.

5. Whisk the yolks into the melted chocolate, then whisk in one-quarter of the meringue. Carefully fold the chocolate mixture into the remaining meringue and fill the tart shells.

6. Bake in the centre of the oven for 7 minutes.

7. Dust with icing sugar and serve immediately with whipped or runny cream, crème fraîche or vanilla ice cream.

COCOA PASTRY **MAKES 550 G**

170 g butter, at room temperature
80 g icing sugar
3 tbsp cocoa powder
1 pinch salt
1 small egg
250 g flour

1. I tend to make this in the food processor, but it can be made by hand. Place the butter, sugar, cocoa and salt in the food processor and blitz for 10 seconds. Scrape the bowl down, then blitz for another 15 seconds until the mixture is creamed.

2. Blitz the egg in, then add the flour all at once and pulse to combine.

3. Take from the processor and gently bring the mixture together on the bench, being careful not to overwork it.

4. Roll into a log about 4 cm in diameter and chill in the fridge for at least 30 minutes. Butter your tart tins and chill in the fridge as well.

5. Instead of rolling out, thinly slice the pastry and layer it into the tins, overlapping the slices like fish scales before pressing flat with floured fingers. Once done, put back in the fridge to chill for another 30 minutes before lining with baking paper and filling with baking beans.

6. Bake at 180°C for 12 minutes, then carefully remove the baking paper and beans and bake for a further 5 minutes.

Melting moments are a biscuit from my childhood, two melt-in-the-mouth biscuits sandwiched together with butter icing. These biscuits, now served as solo biscuits, are a version of those with the addition of ginger chunks, taking them to a more adult level.

GINGER MELTING MOMENTS
MAKES 12–16 BISCUITS

200 g unsalted butter, at room temperature
70 g icing sugar
125 g flour
125 g cornflour
½ tsp baking powder
4 balls candied stem ginger or 6 pieces crystallized ginger, ½ grated and ½ thinly sliced

1. Preheat oven to 170°C. Line a baking tray with baking paper.

2. Cream the butter and icing sugar together.

3. Sift the flours and baking powder and add to the creamed butter to form a dough.

4. Mix in the grated ginger.

5. Take walnut-sized pieces of dough and roll into balls. Place 5 cm apart on the tray. Lay a slice of ginger on top of each one and gently press down with your finger.

6. Bake for 15 minutes. The biscuits should be golden, but not coloured too much.

7. Take from the oven and leave to cool a few minutes before sitting on a cake rack to cool completely. Store in an airtight jar.

Much like a 'brandy snap', these crunchy wafers are best made the day you want to eat them, as they're quite fragile and absorb moisture easily, so keep them in an airtight container once made. They can be rolled around wooden spoon handles to form a cylinder to be piped full of whipped cream or moulded in muffin tins to be used as a basket to serve ice cream and fruit in. The uncooked mixture will keep in the fridge for three weeks.

MANUKA HONEY GINGER SNAPS

MAKES 20 BISCUITS

70 g unsalted butter
40 g manuka honey (or any other honey)
70 g caster sugar
70 g flour
1 tsp ground ginger

1. Heat the butter, honey and sugar over moderate heat in a small pan until the sugar dissolves. Take off the heat and leave to cool for a few minutes.

2. Sift the flour and ginger and mix into the butter. You can either make the snaps immediately or place the cooled mixture in the fridge until needed. When using the mixture from the fridge, let it warm up a little before balling – it'll be easier to handle.

3. Preheat oven to 180°C. Line a baking tray with baking paper.

4. Take marble-sized balls and press them reasonably flat between your fingers, place 10 cm apart on the baking tray and bake until they spread and bubble; for about 8–10 minutes.

5. Leave to cool on the tray for 30 seconds before shaping into cylinders or baskets (see note above recipe). If they become too hard to shape, place back on the tray in the oven to soften them up again.

This is a lovely comforting version of the more familiar summer berry trifle, with the gooseberries adding a tangy sourness to it.

PEAR AND GOOSEBERRY TRIFLE

FOR 8 DESSERTS

400 g slightly stale sponge cake or pound cake (or 30 sponge fingers)

200 ml sweet dessert wine

4 pears, peeled, quartered, cores removed, thickly sliced

300 g gooseberries

4 star anise (or 1½ tsp ground star anise)

300 g sugar

1 litre cream

7 egg yolks

1 tsp vanilla extract

3 tbsp cornflour

3 tbsp icing sugar

100 ml mascarpone or thick Greek-style yoghurt

100 g flaked almonds or macadamias, toasted

1. Cut the cake into fat fingers and scatter two-thirds of them on the bottom of a 2–3 litre heatproof glass bowl. Splash half the wine over the cake and put to one side.

2. Put the pears, gooseberries, star anise and half the sugar in a pan and add half the remaining wine. Put over a moderate high heat and bring to a bubbling mass, stirring constantly. Once it's bubbling, place a lid on and cook for 10 minutes, stirring occasionally, at which point the gooseberries will have burst their skins and the pear will have softened.

3. Pour this over the soaked cake, then scatter the remaining cake on top and drizzle with the remaining wine. Leave to cool, then place in the fridge.

4. Put 750 ml cream in a pan with half the remaining sugar and slowly bring almost to the boil. While it's heating up, whisk the egg yolks with the remaining 75 g sugar and the vanilla until lightened in colour, then whisk in the cornflour. Pour a quarter of the hot cream onto the yolks, whisking as you do, then pour the egg mixture back into the cream. Place back on the heat and cook over a moderate heat until it thickens, whisking constantly.

5. Pour the custard over the sponge in the bowl and leave it to cool, then cover and place in the fridge for at least 4 hours.

6. Thirty minutes before serving, whip the remaining 250 ml cream with the icing sugar and mascarpone or yoghurt to soft peaks, then spread this over the custard and scatter with the toasted nuts. Lightly cover and return to the fridge.

This dairy-rich cheesecake is quite filling, so you get a lot of portions from it. The carrot adds a little flavour and a gorgeous colour. It's best made the day before and just needs serving with whipped cream, yoghurt, fresh fruit or berries.

SPICED CARROT CHEESECAKE
MAKES 1 x 25 cm CHEESECAKE

300 g carrots, peeled, topped and tailed
2 tsp ground cinnamon
2 tsp vanilla extract
1 tsp grated lemon zest
1 x 250 g packet gingernuts or similar
   hard, spiced biscuit
80 g butter, melted
450 g cream cheese
300 g ricotta
140 g crème fraîche
250 g caster sugar
100 g flour, sifted
5 eggs
80 g cream

1. Preheat oven to 150°C. Line the base and sides of a deep 25 cm loose-bottomed cake tin with unbuttered baking paper. Sit the tin on a baking tray with sides, to prevent excess butter running onto the base of your oven.

2. Cut the carrots lengthways, then steam (or boil) until you can easily insert a sharp knife or skewer through them. Drain and leave to cool for 5 minutes.

3. Purée the carrots as smooth as you can in a blender or food processor with the cinnamon, vanilla and lemon zest, and put to one side.

4. In a food processor blitz the gingernuts to coarse crumbs. Add the melted butter and blitz together to fine crumbs. Tip into the base of the prepared tin and press flat.

5. Beat the cream cheese, ricotta and crème fraîche with the sugar until smooth. Beat in the flour, then the eggs, one at a time, allowing them to incorporate after each addition. Beat in the carrot purée, then lastly add the cream.

6. Tip onto the prepared base, place in the lower half of the oven and cook for 1 hour and 10 minutes. Give the cheesecake a half turn halfway through baking.

7. When ready, it should appear as though it's not quite cooked, a little wobbly in the centre but firmish on the outside. If not, then cook for a further 10–20 minutes. Leave to cool, then place in the fridge to firm up.

8. To serve, cut into wedges, remembering it's very rich so you don't need a lot.

This cake is a play on the Egyptian boiled orange and almond cake from my first cookbook – The Sugar Club Cookbook – although it's a little more crumbly due to the texture of the walnuts. I like to serve it with plain yoghurt, crème fraîche or whipped cream.

FLOURLESS LEMON, COCONUT AND WALNUT CAKE

MAKES 1 x 24 cm CAKE (FOR 8-10 PEOPLE)

4 large juicy lemons
250 g runny honey
5 eggs
150 g desiccated coconut
250 g walnuts, roughly chopped
½ tsp vanilla extract
2 tsp baking powder
½ tsp baking soda
1 tsp ground ginger
½ tsp ground nutmeg

1. Preheat oven to 170°C. Line the base and sides of a 24 cm loose-bottomed cake tin with baking paper, but don't grease it.

2. Place 2 lemons in a pot and cover with cold water. Bring to the boil and cook at a rapid simmer with a lid on for 20 minutes, making sure they're floating. Take from the water and leave to cool for 15 minutes. Cut each lemon into quarters and remove seeds. Finely grate the zest from another lemon and place in a food processor with the lemon quarters and 180 g honey. Pulse to a coarse paste.

3. Add the eggs, coconut and half the walnuts and blitz for 10 seconds, scrape down the sides then briefly blitz in the vanilla, baking powder, baking soda and spices. Tip into a bowl and stir in the remaining walnuts.

4. Pour the batter into the tin and bake in the centre of the oven for 30 minutes. A skewer inserted should come out a little moist, but fairly clean.

5. Meanwhile, peel the rind from the remaining lemon and finely julienne it, avoiding the bitter pith. Squeeze the juice from the 2 rindless lemons and put in a small pan with the julienned rind and the remaining 70 g honey. Bring to the boil, then simmer for 5 minutes or so until it becomes a light syrup.

6. Take the cake from the oven, poke it in 20 places with a toothpick or skewer and drizzle with three-quarters of the hot syrup, then leave to cool.

7. Spoon the remaining syrup and julienned rind over as you serve it.

As you'll see in the Breakfast and Brunch chapter in this book, I like to eat baked apples at the start of the day, but also as a dessert on cool nights. Make sure you score the skin before stuffing, as it prevents them from bursting open.

BAKED APPLES WITH PINE NUTS AND VANILLA CUSTARD **FOR 6 DESSERTS**

40 g unsalted butter

40 g brown sugar

1 tbsp pine nuts (or any other nut, roughly chopped)

½ tsp ground spice (cardamom, ginger, allspice, cinnamon or five-spice)

500 ml cream

80 g stale crustless white bread, cut into 1 cm dice

6 Granny Smith apples

70 g caster sugar

¼ vanilla bean, seeds scraped out (or ¼ tsp vanilla paste)

4 egg yolks

1. Preheat oven to 180°C.

2. Place the butter, brown sugar, nuts and spice in a small pan and cook over a moderate heat, stirring frequently, until the nuts are golden and the mixture begins to smell like it is caramelizing. Take off the heat and stir in 100 ml cream and then mix in the bread.

3. Using a small sharp knife, score the skin around the apple (see photo on page 19), avoiding cutting too deeply into the flesh. With their flattest end facing down, remove the seeds and cores (a melon baller is ideal) and place on a baking tray lined with baking paper.

4. Stuff the apples firmly with the filling. Bake for 15–20 minutes, at which point the apples should be cooked (you'll be able to poke a skewer into the centre), and remove from the oven. They can be eaten hot or at room temperature.

5. To make the custard, place the remaining 400 ml cream and half the caster sugar in a pot with the vanilla bean and its seeds (or vanilla paste) and slowly bring almost to the boil. Place the remaining sugar in a bowl with the egg yolks and whisk until pale in colour. Carefully pour on half the hot cream and whisk well, then pour this back into the pot. Cook over a moderate heat, stirring constantly, until it's thick enough to coat the back of a spoon. Take off the heat and pour into a clean bowl, stirring for a minute to help it cool down.

6. To serve, sit a stuffed apple on each plate and pour the custard over and around it.

INDEX